Write It Out

Mastering Short and Extended Responses to Open-Ended Questions

Level G

Coach™
America's Best for Student Success®

Triumph Learning®

About the Authors

Sheila Crowell and *Ellen Kolba* are specialists in the teaching of writing and in preparing students for writing assessments. Their textbooks provide the affirmative support and scaffolding all students need to become better, more confident writers, and to improve their scores on writing assessments.

As staff developers and writing curriculum specialists, Crowell and Kolba show teachers how to evaluate writing by first identifying and specifying the strengths in a draft, then making suggestions based on those strengths to prompt revision. To support the teaching of writing in their own school district in Montclair, New Jersey, they developed *The Writers' Room*™ Program, which trains volunteers from the community, pre-service teachers, and students to serve as writing coaches in elementary, middle, and high school Language Arts and English classes.

Under their direction, *The Writers' Room*™ Program has been brought to schools in Elizabeth, Metuchen, and Trenton, New Jersey, as well as to districts in New York, California, and Canada.

Acknowledgments

Special thanks to our writing team for their
help with this book:

Erin Bad Hand

Caleb E. Crowell

Thomas E. Crowell

Marsha Kalman

Jessica Wade

Song Catcher by Erin Bad Hand. Copyright © 2005.
Used by permission of the author.

Write It Out, Mastering Short and Extended Responses to Open-Ended Questions: Level G

129NA

ISBN-10: 1-59823-030-1
ISBN-13: 978-1-59823-030-7

Authors: Sheila Crowell and Ellen Kolba   Cover Image: Julie Delton/Photodisc/Green/Getty Images

Triumph Learning® 136 Madison Avenue, 7th Floor, New York, NY 10016   © 2007 Triumph Learning, LLC
Kevin McAliley, President and Chief Executive Officer

Printed in the United States of America.

10 9 8 7

Part A: Writing Short Answers

Table of Contents

Part B: Writing Extended Answers

To the Student

In school, you have to take a lot of tests with different types of questions.

One type of test question gives you a list of answers to choose from. You must pick the correct answer from the choices given. Questions like these are called **multiple-choice questions**.

Another type of test question asks you to answer by writing something in your own words. Questions like these, where you write your own answers instead of choosing from a multiple-choice list, are often called **open-ended questions**. They might also be called **constructed-response** or **extended-response questions**. This book is about these kinds of questions.

Open-ended questions are important! An open-ended question counts for more on a test than a multiple-choice question does. So it's important to learn how to write good answers to this kind of question.

Your score on an open-ended question depends on two things:

1) How well you understood the reading selection.

2) How well you expressed your answer in writing.

This book will give you practice doing both.

An open-ended question may call for a short answer or an extended answer.

◉ A short answer contains only a few sentences or a paragraph.

◉ An extended answer may take two paragraphs or more—even a page.

In this book, you will practice writing both short and extended responses to open-ended questions. By the time you get to the end of the book, you should be ready to handle most open-ended questions on a real test.

So let's get started!

5 Rules for Writing Good Answers

This introduction gives you five simple rules to help you write answers to open-ended questions. They are also good rules to follow *whenever* you write.

We call these rules the **SLAMS** rules. At the end of the chapter, you'll see why.

Read the selection on the next two pages. All the questions in the rest of this introduction are about this selection. You may come back to the selection and read it again as often as you like.

Man's Best Friend—the Rat

War is one of the world's great horrors. Not only do people die during a war, but even after a war is officially over. That's because wars leave behind landmines—hidden explosives buried a few inches below the ground. If someone steps on a buried landmine, it explodes. The person either dies or is greatly injured.

Due to wars, between 60 million and 100 million buried landmines exist in many countries around the world that have had a war. These landmines kill or maim more than 25,000 people a year.

The solution, of course, is to find these landmines and get rid of them, but how do you do that? Suppose you are an official, ordered to clear an old minefield. You don't have helicopters that can drag heavy metal mats over the ground to explode hidden mines. You can't afford dogs and their special handlers trained to find landmines, and metal detectors are expensive and not always reliable.

What you need, then, are some *African giant pouched rats*.

Rats? *Giant* rats?

Yes! African giant pouched rats are big critters—about the size of a small cat. They are often kept as pets, since they are both smart and playful. Pet giant rats love to be cuddled, petted, and pampered. They greet people they like with squeaks, chirps, and strange little birdlike noises, called "churbling." They love bananas and peanuts, and they are fond of collecting and hiding small coins, buttons, and other shiny objects. A favorite giant rat posture is sitting upright on its haunches like a squirrel, peering nearsightedly around with its small black eyes, twitching its oversized pink ears, and sniffing in all directions with a long, slightly swollen, pinkish nose that makes the animal look as if it had a cold.

It is this sniffing that makes African giant pouched rats ideal for searching out buried landmines. You see, in the wild, the rats collect food and stuff it in cheek pouches that give the animal its name. They collect more than they can consume at any one time, and they bury the extra food in the ground. Later, their super-sensitive noses help them smell the places where the buried food lies.

In the late 1990s some scientists in Belgium reasoned that African giant pouched rats might be trained to find landmines. They hoped the animals could smell the small amounts of vapor given off by TNT, the explosive chemical used in the landmines. Using training techniques pioneered by the American psychologist B. F. Skinner, the scientists took young giant pouched rats and exposed them to the smell of buried TNT. If the animals sat down or scratched at the ground near the TNT, they were rewarded with food. Gradually, the animals learned that if they sat and scratched at the ground whenever they smelled TNT, they would be rewarded with a peanut or a bite of banana. As the animals got better at their task, the amounts of TNT were gradually reduced until the animals were able to smell even a tiny amount of TNT vapor given off by a buried landmine.

Some animals were more skilled than others. These talented rats were specially bred, and their children were trained and tested in turn. In early tests, a rat named Julie scored 100%, and her friend Bean was nearly as good. Dina and Bianca, on the other hand, never really caught on. You can guess which rats were chosen for the breeding program. After several generations, the rats became natural landmine sniffers. Mother rats were even training their offspring!

When the giant rats were tested on real minefields, they were a huge success. Along one stretch of railroad they found twenty buried mines, any one of which could have been set off by the rattle of a passing train.

Scientists are finding other jobs for these talented rats, too. They are using giant rats to help doctors detect the deadly lung disease TB. TB, or tuberculosis, kills about 2 million people a year worldwide, and the death toll is expected to rise to 8 million a year by the end of the next decade.

Usually, lab technicians identify the illness by looking through a microscope at the patient's saliva and searching for the bacteria that cause the disease. But African giant pouched rats can be trained to smell the disease just by sniffing at a saliva sample. As a result, they work much faster than people can. A human technician can examine only about twenty saliva samples in a day. In an hour, a rat can screen 300 samples! The rat-sniff test may soon become the fastest way of finding out whether a patient has TB or not.

The African giant pouched rat may never replace the dog as a person's best animal friend, but in many places around the world, it is coming in a close second!

Rule 1: Sentences

Here is an open-ended question you might find on a test:

> **According to the selection, what can African giant pouched rats be used for?**

Bonnie's answer:

finding mines

Bonnie's answer is correct. Nevertheless, she probably would not get a good score on a test. Her answer is not written in a complete sentence.

> **Rule 1:** Answers to open-ended questions should always be written in complete sentences! (Exception: When you fill out a chart.)

Bonnie's answer would have been better if she had written it like this:

Scientists have found that African giant pouched rats can be used to sniff out buried landmines. The rats have a very keen sense of smell and can be trained to find mines buried in the ground.

Now suppose a test question asked this:

> **How dangerous are landmines?**

Angela's answer:

very dangerous

Rewrite Angela's answer so that it would get a better score:

_____

_____

_____

When you come across an open-ended question on a test, you probably wonder how much you should write. Here's a good rule to remember.

> **Rule 2:** **The number of lines on the test is a rough guide for how long your answer should be.**

If your handwriting is big, you'll need about one and a half lines to write a sentence. If you write small, you'll need only one line for a sentence.

✓ So, if you see four or five lines, you should probably write about three or four sentences.

✓ If you see a whole page of lines, you should probably write one or two paragraphs.

✓ If you see two full pages of lines, then you should write three or more paragraphs.

Shaun read this question on a test:

How do African giant pouched rats differ from ordinary rats?

Shaun's Answer:

They are *bigger* and have *pouches*.

_____

_____

_____

Shaun's answer is correct, but it is too short. He should add more details from the selection.

On the lines after Shaun's answer, add more details that tell how African giant pouched rats differ from ordinary rats. Remember to write your answer in complete sentences.

_____

_____

_____

Rule 3: Answer the Question

Rule 3: Answer the question that the test asks!

Rule 3 may seem logical and easy to do, but you must be careful. Many students get into trouble because they forget or don't understand what the question asked. They write about a similar topic, but they don't actually answer the right question. You must read the question carefully and write only information that answers the question. Don't give lots of information about other things that don't answer it. For example, read this question:

> **In the wild, what do the giant rats use their noses for?**

Malcolm's Answer:

> The giant rats have super-sensitive noses. They can smell things you and I could never smell. We can only smell strong things, like burning toast or an apple pie cooking in the oven. But the giant rats can smell much, much *better* than that.

Dave's Answer:

> The giant rats use their super-sensitive noses to sniff out buried food. They collect food in their cheek pouches and then bury it. Then, when they get hungry, they use their noses to sniff out the buried food.

The information in both answers is true, but Malcolm's answer doesn't answer what the question asks.

✓ Most of Malcolm's facts are not from the selection.

✓ The question does not ask students to compare the smelling ability of rats with that of humans, which is what Malcolm wrote about.

Dave's answer is better. He answers the question that was asked.

> **Why do African giant pouched giant rats make good pets?**

Try it. Answer the question, using the information in the selection:

_____

_____

_____

_____

When writers—or teachers—say "mechanics," they don't mean people who fix cars. In writing, mechanics means spelling, punctuation, and capitalization. Mechanics also means correct grammar and good word choices.

> **Rule 4:** **Mechanics are important! Your answer should have no mistakes.**

You won't get a low score on open-ended questions if you write good answers with just a few minor mistakes in spelling or usage. If you aren't careful, though, and your answer has several mistakes, you will lose points.

How can African giant rats help in the fight against TB?

Consuela's Answer:

The afracan giant rats can *be* used in labs to identify the spit from a person who has TB they can *be* traned to spot the smell of spit. From a TB pashunt. A human with a micriscope can only looked at 20 spit samples a day. But a giant rat can sniff 300 spit samples an hour.

Consuela's answer has a lot of information, but she would have gotten a much better score if she had paid attention to mechanics. Her answer has:

✓ 4 spelling errors

✓ 1 run-on sentence and 1 sentence fragment

✓ 3 mistakes in capitalization (1 because of the run-on sentence, 1 because of the fragment)

✓ 1 mistake in verb tense

Rewrite Consuela's answer with no mistakes. (HINT: All the misspelled words can be found in the selection, spelled correctly.)

_____

_____

_____

_____

_____

Rule 5: Support Your Answer

This may be the most important rule of all. It's especially important because many students don't apply this rule when they write responses to open-ended questions.

> **Rule 5:** **Support your answers with details from the selection!**

Support means to include information that explains or adds to your answer. Supporting details make your answer complete.

✓ For some questions, some or all of the support for your answers must come from the reading selection you are reading.

✓ For other questions, it is okay to add your own opinions, but you MUST include some information from the selection, no matter what you write.

For example, read this question and the student answers that follow.

> **In training, were all the rats equally good at sniffing out buried TNT?**

Pat's Answer:

No. Some rats were no good.

Shivaun's Answer:

In training, some rats were better than others at sniffing out buried TNT. The rat named Julie got a perfect score, and a rat named Bean was also very good. The rats named Dina and Bianca never did well.

Vince's Answer:

Some rats were not as good as other rats. Maybe they were just not naturally good sniffers, or maybe something was wrong with their noses. Or maybe they were good sniffers, but just couldn't be trained.

How do you think each student scored? Draw a line between each student's name and the description of his or her answer.

Pat   WEAK.   Supporting details don't come from the slection.

Shivaun   WEAK.   Not enough supporting details.

Vince   GOOD!   Supports answer with details from the selection.

Try it. Read and answer the following question. Be sure to look back at the selection for details to support your answer.

How did the scientists train the African giant pouched rats to find buried landmines?

Write your answer here.

_____
_____
_____
_____
_____
_____
_____
_____
_____
_____
_____
_____

SLAMS—A Memory Gem

To help you remember the five rules in this chapter, remember this word: SLAMS!

stands for **S**entence. Write your answers in complete sentences.

stands for **L**ines. The number of lines on the answer sheet gives you an idea of how long your answer should be.

stands for **A**nswer. Answer the question that the test asks. Answer all parts of the question. Read the question a few times to make sure you understand what the question asks.

stands for **M**echanics. Mechanics are punctuation, capitalization, spelling, grammar, and usage. Your sentence mechanics should be correct. You should write without mistakes.

stands for **S**upport. Remember to support your answer with details from the selection.

When you answer open-ended questions, try to recall this memory gem. Give your answers the *SLAMS* test. If your answer doesn't follow all of the *SLAMS* rules, fix it!

Remember—a good answer **SLAMS** the question!

Scoring Rubric

Every test has a different way of scoring the answers to an open-ended question. One of the most common methods is a scale of **0 to 4**. The **highest score** is a **4**; the **lowest score** is a **0**.

It might help if you know what you need to get a **4** or a **3**. Here are some rubric guidelines for answering open-ended questions.

SCORE	WHAT IT MEANS

 4

You answered the question clearly and completely.

You included ideas from the reading selection that are on target.

You supported these ideas with details and examples.

If the question asked you to, you connected the ideas from the reading selection to your own ideas and experiences.

You answered in complete and interesting sentences.

 3

You answered the question.

You included some ideas from the reading selection.

You used some examples and details for support.

If the question asked you to, you connected some of the ideas from the reading selection to your own experiences.

Most of your sentences were complete.

 2

You only answered part of the question.

You only included one or two ideas or details from the reading selection. The main ideas may not have been included.

You didn't connect your own ideas or experiences with the reading passage.

Many of your sentences were written incorrectly.

 1

You didn't seem to understand the reading selection.

Your answer didn't include the important details from the selection.

You didn't connect your ideas to the reading passage.

You often wrote only single words or groups of words instead of complete sentences.

 0

You didn't write anything; OR

You didn't answer the question asked.

Part A

Writing Short Answers

Fact and Opinion

If you look at your local paper, you will find two types of articles.

On the first page you might read an article about an upcoming election in your town. The *reporter* mentions all the candidates, and she describes their qualifications and their previous voting records on certain issues. The article might even include a chart that makes it easier for readers to compare the candidates.

On the *editorial page*, however, you find another article about the election. In this article, the writer endorses one of the candidates. He gives all the reasons why that candidate is the best choice. If he discusses the other candidates at all, he does it only to illustrate why his candidate is better.

What's going on here? Aren't newspaper reporters supposed to be objective? Aren't they supposed to write the *who-what-when-where and why* of a story? The reporter of the front-page article did just that. She reported the **facts** of the story. Facts are information that can be proven *true* or *false*.

An *editorial writer*, however, is supposed to *interpret the facts and express an* **opinion**. In this example, the writer used facts to reach his own opinion about the best candidate. Readers may *agree* or *disagree* with his opinion, but they cannot say that his opinion is right or wrong.

At school, you are given different writing assignments. For your science teacher, you may have to write a research paper, full of facts. Your social studies teacher, on the other hand, may ask you to express an opinion on a controversial issue. A good writer must know how to do both, and a good reader must be able to distinguish *fact* from *opinion*.

Lesson 1

What Makes a Good Answer?

Read this selection. It includes both facts and opinions. The question that follows asks you to find the facts.

Speaking Without Words

Think about a time when a teacher asked you to do something you didn't want to do. You didn't want to hurt the teacher's feelings or risk detention by talking back, but you let your feelings show anyway. Maybe you rolled your eyes. Maybe you made a face, or pointed a finger to your head and moved it in circles to show that you thought the teacher was crazy to make that request. Even though you didn't say anything, everyone still knew what you meant.

This paragraph is loaded with facts.

Words aren't the only way that people communicate. Even when we don't say anything, we express more than we realize. The gestures we make with our hands, our facial expressions, the way we hold our bodies, even the way we dress and wear our hair all contribute to how we communicate information about ourselves. This kind of nonverbal communication is known as body language.

We can't always control our body language. Some body language is involuntary. Did you ever try to stop blushing when you were embarrassed? Can you keep from jumping in fright when someone sneaks up on you? These reactions are *innate*. We are born with them, and we respond *instinctively*.

Look for a fact about the military here.

Other nonverbal signals are learned. In the military, for example, new recruits quickly learn to salute to show respect for superior officers. Learned signals are not universal. They mean different things in different cultures. In the United States, we learn to clap our hands to show that we appreciate a concert or a show. In some European countries, the people in the audience may stamp their feet to show the same appreciation.

Some body language combines the learned and the innate. Everybody is born knowing how to cry. In fact, crying is one of the first ways a baby communicates with the world. As we grow up, the culture we live in teaches us when it is appropriate to cry, and when we should hold back our tears.

Because people "listen" to conversations with their eyes as well as their ears, unspoken signals can clarify our spoken words. They also can lead to confusion. Sometimes our facial expression says one thing but our words say the opposite. When we send a "mixed signal," the person we are speaking with can easily become confused. Then body language may become more important than the words. The message that comes through more clearly is the one that our body language conveys.

Nonverbal communication can lead to serious misunderstandings. Diplomats, business people, and even vacation travelers need to know that the meaning of body language varies from culture to culture. Something as simple as sitting down and putting your feet up may be perfectly acceptable in this country. In other countries, however, showing the soles of your shoes is considered a grave insult. Handshaking is another example. Americans believe that a firm handshake conveys confidence. People in Asia interpret a firm handshake as a sign of aggression.

Despite cultural differences in interpreting body language, one nonverbal sign is universal. You may not speak someone's language. You may not know how to signal that you lost your suitcase or that you need a piece of paper. What you can do is smile. A sincere *smile* conveys the same message everywhere in the world. It's the quickest way to turn strangers into friends.

What fact is this paragraph about?

Why is it important to be aware of body language? Use facts from the selection to support your answer.

Rory's Answer:

Rory wrote a good answer to this question. Read what she wrote, then answer the questions that follow. They will help you understand what made her answer so successful.

It is important to be aware of body language because people communicate with more than words. We also "speak" with our hands, our posture, our eyes, and our facial expressions. We are born with some body language that we cannot control, like blushing when we are embarrassed. We learn other kinds of body language, like when a new recruit learns to salute an officer in the military. Some of our body language is a combination. We all know how to cry when we are born, but when we get older, we are taught when it is okay to cry and when we should hold it in. We learn how to express our feelings in a way that is acceptable in our culture.

Body language can mean different things in different societies. Something that is okay to do in the United States might offend people in another country. For example, we think it is okay to put our feet up when we are relaxing in a chair. In other countries, though, showing the soles of our feet is an insulting gesture. If we want to avoid misunderstandings, we have to be aware of the things we "say" with our gestures, as well as with our words.

HINT!

Test scorers look for the following elements in an answer:

* A clear statement of the main idea.

* A clear understanding of the difference between fact and opinion.

* Facts from the selection to develop and support the answer.

* Complete, correct, and interesting sentences.

What Makes Rory's Answer Work?

To see what makes a successful response, let's take a closer look at Rory's answer.

1. Rory starts with a sentence that states the main idea of her answer. She uses the words of the question in her opening sentence. This helps keep her answer focused. Rory also includes an important fact that she learned from the reading selection. This fact is the main idea.

   What is Rory's opening sentence? Write it here. Underline the fact that provides the main idea of her answer.

   _____

   _____

   _____

2. Rory supports her answer with facts from the reading selection. In her first paragraph, she discusses the different kinds of body language. Here is how she identifies one kind of body language: "We are born with some body language that we cannot control, like blushing when we are embarrassed."

   What other two types of body language does Rory include in her first paragraph? Write Rory's sentences here.

   _____

   _____

   _____

   _____

3. In her second paragraph, Rory discusses how the same body language can mean different things in different cultures. She uses an example from the reading selection to support her answer.

   What example does Rory include to show cultural differences in interpreting body language? Write Rory's example here.

   _____

   _____

   _____

   _____

4. Rory's conclusion expands on the ideas expressed in her opening sentence.

How does Rory conclude her answer? Write Rory's conclusion here.

_____

_____

_____

5. Rory writes sentences that are clear, correct, and interesting. Here is one example: "We all know how to cry when we are born, but when we get older, we are taught when it is okay to cry and when we should hold it in."

Find another of Rory's sentences that is clear, correct, and interesting. Write Rory's sentence here.

_____

_____

_____

_____

_____

_____

Tools & Tips

Distinguishing between *fact* and *opinion* can be challenging. Compare the following two examples.

A. I think everyone should be required to study Spanish in school. Spanish is the second most commonly spoken language in the United States.

B. I think everyone should be required to study Spanish in school. Spanish is the most beautiful language in the world.

Both examples begin with the same opinion. In example A, the second sentence is a fact that supports the opinion. The fact makes the opinion more convincing. In example B, the second sentence looks like a fact, but it isn't. The words *most beautiful* are a clue. How can you measure how beautiful a language is? You can't. It is an opinion. It doesn't support the opinion in the first sentence.

To distinguish between fact and opinion, you must realize that:

Facts can be checked. For example:
- Five foreign languages are offered at my middle school.
- Mr. Medina studied in Italy.
- _____

Add another fact to this list on the line above.

Opinions cannot be checked. For example:
- French is the most useful language to study.
- Mr. Medina is the best teacher in the district.
- _____

Add another opinion to this list on the line above.

28

Lesson 2

Revising and Improving a Weak Answer

Now read this selection. The question that follows on *page 30* asks for an opinion. Your opinion should be supported by facts from the text and by personal experience.

A Different Kind of Language

Did you ever turn off the sound when you were watching a show on television? Were you still able to understand everything that was happening? Could you tell when something funny or something sad occurred? Did you feel that you were missing large parts of the story?

Most of us rely on spoken words to communicate and understand. However, while we talk, we don't just stand rigidly at attention. Our bodies also do some "talking." Hand movements and facial expressions accompany our speech. Our body language helps listeners understand what we are trying to say. That is why when you watch actors on television, you can still partially understand what is happening, even with the sound turned off.

Facts about sign language first appear here.

Even so, life can be very confusing when you cannot hear what is happening around you. Imagine, therefore, how much more important body language becomes to people who cannot hear. Many deaf and hearing-impaired people, as well as hearing people who want to communicate with the hearing-impaired, use a special, learned body language called **sign language**. Sign language is a silent form of communication based entirely on *gestures* and *visual cues*.

Facts about specific languages appear here.

Most people believe that there is just one universal sign language. Like spoken language, however, sign language varies from culture to culture. Throughout the world, people use over 200 distinct forms of sign language. Chinese signers, for example, cannot understand French Sign Language any more than Chinese speakers can comprehend the spoken French language. In fact, separate sign languages exist even in countries with a common language. For example, people in the United States and in Great Britain mostly speak English. However American Sign Language (ASL) is a quite different from British Sign Language.

Sign language is not merely a translation of words into gestures. It is a language based on concepts and ideas. It also has its own grammar rules that differ from those of spoken English. Hand gestures, facial expressions, posture, and the space around the signer are the building blocks of the language. The manual alphabet (or finger spelling to spell words letter by letter) supplements sign language. Finger spelling is used only when there is no equivalent sign for a specific word, such as a person's name. Even with finger spelling, there are cultural differences. For instance, British finger spellers use both hands to form words, while Americans use only one hand.

An early form of American Sign Language was used as far back as colonial times. When Thomas Gallaudet opened the first American school for the deaf in 1817, he hired a deaf teacher named Laurent Clerc. Because Clerc was a Parisian, he used French Sign Language. The earlier American form of sign language and the French version that he taught his students combined to become modern American Sign Language. Today ASL is a full, rich language that conveys the folklore, history, and culture of the deaf community in America.

Nearly half a million people employ American Sign Language as their primary language. In fact, ASL is the fourth most commonly "spoken" language in North America. ASL even fulfills the foreign-language requirement of many high schools and colleges. It is treated just like Spanish, German, or French. The number of people who use American Sign Language is growing every day.

Learn how ASL first developed here.

Should American Sign Language be accepted as the foreign-language requirement in high schools and colleges? What is your opinion? Give reasons for your opinion, using details from the selection and your personal experience to support your answer.

Dean's Answer:

Dean wrote an answer, but it was not a very good one. Can you figure out why? Read his answer below.

American Sign Language is really cool. We had an assembly at school last week where there was a sign language interpreter on the side of the stage. She was there to translate what the speakers said into sign language. The way she used her hands and arms was awesome. It was hard to concentrate on the speakers because what she was doing was so interesting. Of course, the speakers were pretty boring. Assemblies always are boring. I usually goof around with my friends. Sometimes we get detention but it's worth it.

Improving Dean's Answer

Dean's answer would not get a good score. He gave his opinion about American Sign Language, but he did not answer the question. Dean supported his opinion with some interesting details from his personal experience, but he did not include any information from the reading selection. Then toward the end of his answer, he lost focus. The last four sentences aren't related to the topic at all. To improve his answer, he needs to answer the question clearly and completely.

HINT!

The test scorers look for the following elements:

✔ A clear statement of your opinion.

✔ Evidence that you clearly understand the difference between facts and opinions.

✔ Facts from the selection to support the answer.

✔ Complete, correct, and interesting sentences.

Use the following questions to help you improve Dean's answer.

1. Dean needs an opening sentence that answers the question and helps him stay on topic. One way to do this is to restate the question in the first sentence.

   Rewrite Dean's opening sentence. Write the new sentence here.

   _____

   _____

   _____

2. Dean needs to support his opinion with facts from the reading selection. For example, he could start by saying that ASL is a language of its own, not just a silent form of English.

   Find more facts in the reading selection that show why ASL is a distinct language. Write at least three new sentences to support Dean's opinion.

   _____

   _____

   _____

   _____

3. Dean's answer should be longer. A good answer should be at least two paragraphs long. He should start his second paragraph with a smooth transition to tie his ideas together.

   How can Dean connect the ideas in his two paragraphs? Write two transition sentences for the second paragraph. The first sentence should relate back to the facts in the first paragraph. The second sentence should tie into Dean's personal experience.

   _____

   _____

   _____

   _____

4. In the second paragraph, Dean should use details from his own experience to support his opinion. This kind of support will make his answer more personal and show that he can relate the question to real life.

Go back to Dean's original answer. Find details from his own experience to further support his opinion. Write three sentences to further support Dean's opinion with details from his own experience.

_____

_____

_____

_____

_____

_____

5. Dean needs a clear and convincing end to his answer. A strong conclusion brings the reader back to the main idea in an interesting way.

How can Dean tie his ideas together in a convincing and interesting way? Write a closing sentence for Dean's answer here.

_____

_____

_____

SCORE BUILDER

Before you forget—

What is the memory gem word?

_____

What does each letter stand for?

1 _____

_____

_____

2 _____

_____

_____

3 _____

_____

_____

4 _____

_____

_____

5 _____

_____

_____

34

Lesson 3

Responding on Your Own

The final selection in this unit discusses the possibility of a universal language. The question that follows asks you to express and explain your opinion.

One World, One Language

Saluton!

Someday soon, this simple word might be the way you greet people around the world. What does it mean? *Saluton* means hello in Esperanto, a new universal language.

Every year, more and more Americans travel outside the United States. Satellites make it possible for us to see television programs from around the world. The Internet allows us to share information with people in other countries. There's just one problem: How can people who speak different languages understand each other?

In 1887, a physician in Poland, Dr. Ludwig L. Zamenhof, came up with a solution to this dilemma. He invented a new language. Dr. Zamenhof called his new language Esperanto, which means one who hopes. He hoped to create a simple way for people to communicate freely and easily, no matter where in the world they lived. Although Esperanto may not have caught on at the level Dr. Zamenhof anticipated, many people have adopted his dream. By some estimates, about two million people around the world speak Esperanto today, about the same number of people who speak Hebrew or Lithuanian.

With 16 basic rules of grammar, Esperanto is one of the easiest languages to learn. The grammar rules are easy to follow, with no variations. For example, Spanish, French, and English have irregular verbs—verbs that follow rules different from most verbs in the language. Esperanto doesn't have irregular verbs. Because Esperanto is based largely on Latin, French, German, or English roots, newcomers to Esperanto can build their vocabularies fairly quickly. Knowledge of Esperanto may even make it easier to learn other foreign languages.

Esperanto is easy to speak, too, because it is a phonetic language. Each of the 28 letters in the Esperanto alphabet has one specific sound. The letter *g* always sounds like the *g* in garden. The letter *e* always is short, like the *e* in *red*. There is only one way to spell a word, and one way to pronounce it. Esperanto words are always accented on the next-to-last syllable.

Although Esperanto may not have achieved the goals set by its creator, it is very much a living language. Thousands of people around the world today

What do you learn about Esperanto here?

How is Esperanto like other languages? How is it different?

speak Esperanto. Esperantists hold annual conventions in locations as diverse as Beijing, China, and Austin, Texas. Professional organizations cater to teachers, doctors, and journalists who speak Esperanto, as well as Esperantists who share an interest in hobbies like stamp collecting. Young people who want to find out more about Esperanto or meet others interested in the language can join Tutmonda Esperantista Junulara Organizo, the World Esperanto Youth Organization

As with any language, a wide variety of literature is available in Esperanto. Many books have been written in Esperanto, and even more have been translated into the language. You can find everything from the complete works of William Shakespeare to current magazines in Esperanto. Esperanto shows up in movies, too. Directors who want to represent bilingual cultures in their films frequently choose Esperanto as the second language for their characters. Even video games come in Esperanto.

Esperanto is a "foreign" language for everyone. It does not replace a speaker's native language or make one language any more important than another. By breaking down language barriers, Esperanto plays an important role in promoting global understanding.

Ĉu vi parolas Esperanton? That means, "Do you speak Esperanto?" You just might want to give it a try!

What do you learn about Esperanto worldwide?

What facts and opinions are expressed here?

Do you think that if everyone spoke Esperanto, the world would be a better place? Why do you think that? Explain your opinion. Support your opinion with facts from all three reading selections in this unit, as well as your own experience.

Write your answer on the lines below.

_____

_____

_____

_____

_____

_____

_____

_____

_____

_____

_____

_____

_____

_____

_____

_____

_____

HINT!

When you are finished, check your answer:

✔ Have you expressed your opinion clearly?

✔ Have you supported your opinion with facts from the reading selections and from your own experience?

✔ Does your answer meet the SLAMS tests?

Reader's Response
Revise & Edit

When you have finished writing, exchange papers with a partner. As you read each other's answers, follow these steps.

1 Did the writer fully answer the question asked?   ___ **Yes** ___ **No**
If not, what needs to be added or changed?
Write your response here.

_____

_____

_____

2 Did the writer use facts from the selections   ___ **Yes** ___ **No**
and from personal experience to support the answer?
If not, what needs to be added or changed?
Write your response here.

_____

_____

_____

3 Was the answer clear and easy to understand?   ___ **Yes** ___ **No**

4 Did the writer use a variety of sentences?   ___ **Yes** ___ **No**

5 Has the writer followed all the SLAMS rules?   ___ **Yes** ___ **No**
If not, which rules were not followed?
Check all the boxes that apply.

S ___   L ___   A ___   M ___   S ___

6 **Give the paper back to your partner to revise and edit.**

Reviewing the Question

Make sure you know how to distinguish *fact* from *opinion*.

- A **fact** can be checked. You can look it up to make sure that it is correct.

- An **opinion** cannot be checked. It is a *personal interpretation of facts*. A **persuasive opinion** must be *backed up with facts*. Although an opinion cannot be right or wrong, it won't be very convincing if it is based on faulty thinking.

Many reading selections contain a mix of facts and opinions. Different school assignments will require you to include facts and opinions. It is important to know when facts are needed and when it is appropriate to give your opinion.

Cause and Effect

Turn the key in the ignition switch of a car. The car starts.

Put a pan full of dough into a hot oven. An hour later, you have a loaf of bread.

Hit a baseball out of the park in the bottom of the ninth inning of a tied ball game. Your team wins the game.

These examples demonstrate cause and effect.

🌀 An *action* that makes something happen is called a **cause**. You turn the key. You bake the dough. You hit the baseball. Each action causes something to happen.

🌀 An **effect** is that *result*. Because you turned the key, the car starts. The dough becomes bread after it is baked in a hot oven. Your team wins because you hit the ball out of the park.

Of course, cause and effect is not always that straightforward. One cause may lead to several effects. For example, suppose you oversleep for school. That single event may cause you to skip breakfast, get to school late, and miss an important exam.

Similarly, one effect may be the result of multiple causes. The Civil War was not fought solely to abolish slavery. Economic and states' rights issues also were important causes of the war.

Lesson 4

What Makes a Good Answer?

Read the nonfiction selection below. The question that follows deals with the role women played during the Revolutionary War.

Revolutionary Women

Women in colonial America had few legal or political rights. They were expected to take care of the home and the family and leave national concerns to the men. These limited rights, however, did not keep colonial women from expressing their opinions or from acting on their beliefs.

This paragraph tells something that women could still do.

Abigail Adams wrote many letters to her husband, John, during his long absences from home. In her letters, she never hesitated to let him know how she felt about the important issues of the day. When he became president, many of his policies reflected her insights and ideas. Another influential woman, Mercy Otis Warren, was known as the "Conscience of the Revolution." She hosted political gatherings and wrote pamphlets and satirical, anti-British plays. In 1805, she published a three-volume history about the Revolutionary War.

The next two paragraphs tell how women got around the laws.

Women had to be creative to get around the rules that kept them from joining in the struggle against British rule. Some women followed their husbands into battle and fought at their sides. Margaret Cochran Corbin's husband was killed during the Battle of Fort Washington in 1776. After taking over his position, "Captain Molly" was wounded and taken prisoner. Her bravery earned her a military pension, awarded by Congress in 1779. Mary Ludwig Hays, who earned the nickname "Molly Pitcher" by carrying water to the troops during battle, also took over her husband's duties when he was wounded during the Battle of Monmouth in 1778.

A number of women went one step further. They disguised themselves as men so they could join the army. One such woman was Deborah Sampson. Her first attempt to pass herself off as a man failed, but she didn't let that stop her. She was determined to be a soldier. When she tried to enlist a second time, she succeeded. As Robert Shurtleff, she served in the colonial army for more than a year. Wounded twice in battle, she received an honorable discharge from the army after a doctor discovered her true identity.

How did this woman's traditional role help the war?

Some colonial women let their gender work to their advantage. They became spies. "Mom" Rinker ran a tavern in British-occupied Philadelphia. Drunken soldiers paid little attention to the woman who served them their tankards of ale every night. Because they did not notice her, she was able to overhear a great deal of valuable military information. When she spent her days knitting in a nearby park, no one paid much attention to her there, either. The British never realized that she hid messages about their plans in balls of wool, which she periodically dropped to patriots waiting in the woods below her rocky perch at the park.

In extraordinary times, even the most ordinary activity can take on a whole new meaning. Many colonial women turned their daily chores into acts of rebellion. For example, to support their colony's boycott of tea and other British imports, they experimented with new ways to make drinks from local plants to replace tea. A group of women in North Carolina even held their own "tea party." Boston women gathered with their spinning wheels. They worked together to make fabric to ease the shortage caused by the colonists' refusal to buy British products.

Armed with muskets, quill pens, or knitting needles, colonial women played an important role in the Revolutionary War. Generations of American women, from the Civil War through the civil rights movement and on into the twenty-first century, have followed in their footsteps.

Look for two ways women's traditional tasks helped the war.

Colonial American women had very few legal and political rights. What effect did the women's status have on their participation in the Revolutionary War? Use details from the selection and your own ideas to support your answer.

Desmond's Answer:

Desmond wrote a good answer to this question. Read what he wrote. Then answer the questions that follow. They will help you understand what makes his answer so successful.

Women in colonial America did not have many legal or political rights. They were expected to stay at home and take care of their families. This meant that they had to find creative ways to participate in the struggle for independence.

Women who followed the rules and stayed home turned their daily chores into rebellious acts. They spun their own cloth. They learned to make tea from local plants. Every time they found substitutes for boycotted British products they helped defeat the British.

Many women wanted to do even more. Mercy Otis Warren wrote anti-British plays. Some women followed their husbands into battle and fought alongside them, like "Captain Molly" Cochran. Some disguised themselves as men so they could enlist in the army. Deborah Sampson was a soldier for more than a year and was wounded two times. Some women were spies, like "Mom" Rinker. She was able to find out military secrets because British soldiers didn't pay attention to her when they went to her tavern.

Colonial women found many ways to join the fight for independence. They figured out how to overcome the limits that were placed on them so that they could help win independence for the United States.

HINT!

The test scorers look for the following elements:

✔ A clear statement of the answer.

✔ A clear understanding of cause and effect.

✔ Facts from the selection that support the answer.

✔ Complete, correct, and interesting sentences.

What Makes Desmond's Answer Work?

Let's take a closer look at Desmond's answer.

1. Desmond starts with a sentence that shows he understands the legal and political status of colonial women. Then he includes a fact from the reading selection that supports his opening sentence.

   What fact from the selection does Desmond use for support? Write his sentence here.

   _____

   _____

   _____

2. Instead of answering the question directly in his first sentence, Desmond waits until the end of his opening paragraph. He builds his answer by giving supporting information first. This technique is a good way to get the reader's attention because it is unusual. (Usually, the answer comes before the supporting details.)

   In which sentence does Desmond answer the question? Write Desmond's answer here.

   _____

   _____

3. In the second paragraph, Desmond provides specific examples from the selection to show how colonial women participated in the American Revolution. Here is the opening sentence of the second paragraph: "Women who followed the rules and stayed home turned their daily chores into rebellious acts."

   What specific examples does Desmond provide in the rest of this paragraph? Write two of Desmond's sentences here.

   _____

   _____

   _____

   _____

   _____

4. In the third paragraph, Desmond includes examples to show how colonial women participated in the American Revolution. Here is the opening sentence of Desmond's third paragraph: "Many women wanted to do even more."

   What specific examples does Desmond include in this paragraph? Write two of Desmond's sentences here.

   _____

   _____

   _____

   _____

   _____

5. Desmond starts his closing paragraph, or conclusion, with a generalization that ties together his examples.

   a. **What generalization does Desmond make? Write his sentence here.**

   _____

   _____

   _____

6. Desmond writes a final sentence that expresses a more personal interpretation of his answer.

   b. **What is Desmond's personal interpretation? Write his sentence here.**

   _____

   _____

Tools & Tips

When instructions ask you to "use examples from your own experience," does your mind go blank? Do you find it hard to make connections with something that happened in the past or to adults? Think again! You have many experiences that you can relate to topics that may be new today. You gain this experience through different sources. Here are some non-school sources through which you might gain personal knowledge and experience:

- ✓ conversations with friends or family members
- ✓ books and magazines
- ✓ song lyrics
- ✓ the Internet
- ✓ movies, TV, and radio

You build experiences and knowledge not only through the things you do, but through the things you see, hear, and read. You just have to know how to recognize the experiences—and use them!

Think about the things you read, see, hear, and learn that can broaden your experiences. List them on the lines below.

_____

_____

_____

_____

_____

_____

_____

_____

_____

_____

Lesson 5

Revising and Improving a Weak Answer

Here is another nonfiction reading selection. The question that follows asks you to consider some of the results of the Revolutionary War.

Liberty and Justice for All?

The Revolutionary War, or the American Revolution, did not bring independence to everyone in the new nation. African American patriots fought bravely in the hope that the new nation would abolish slavery. Native American tribes wanted to keep the lands where they had always lived. The end of the war, however, did not bring either group the benefits they sought.

What were African Americans' rights?

Crispus Attucks, an African American man, was the first person to die in the battle that started the Revolutionary War, the Battle of Lexington. After his death, other African Americans eagerly joined the fight. They served in integrated units at Concord, Lexington, and Bunker Hill. Black or white, all soldiers received the same pay.

Then attitudes changed. Wealthy landowners, especially in the southern colonies, feared British rule, but they feared a slave revolt even more. Cotton and tobacco, their main crops, required a lot of land and a lot of manual labor. Landowners felt they could not productively run their plantations without slaves.

Look for how these rights changed and why.

The British took advantage of the situation. They encouraged the slaveholders' fears. At the same time, they lured slaves to their cause with the promise of freedom. About 1,000 African Americans enlisted as soldiers in the British army. Thousands more worked as cooks, nurses, and laborers. When the British were defeated, 20,000 blacks left the United States. Some went to England or Canada. Others settled in the West Indies or in Sierra Leone in western Africa. Despite the promises they had made, the British also sold some African Americans back into slavery.

Because of pressure from the slaveholders, George Washington had forced African-American soldiers to leave the Continental Army. Faced with the British effort to recruit black soldiers, however, Washington soon reversed his policy. By the end of the war, at least 5,000 African Americans, mainly from the North, had fought with the rebels. By 1804, all of the Northern states had abolished slavery, but the war did not have the same effect in the South.

Much of what we know today about African American soldiers comes from a book published in 1855 by William Cooper Nell, an African American lawyer and abolitionist from Boston. *Colored Patriots of the American Revolution* was the first, and probably the most complete, record of the African Americans who fought for independence. Thanks to Nell's research, we know the story of Salem Poor, the only man singled out for praise as a "brave and gallant soldier" at the Battle of Charlestown. We also know about James Armistead Lafayette, one of the most important American spies, and James Forten, a prisoner of war who rejected an offer to live in England as a free man.

Native Americans also took part in the American Revolution. They did not fight because they believed in the rights of the British Empire, nor did they fight because they believed in the democratic ideas of the American republic. Rather, they fought only when they could no longer remain neutral. They fought to protect their homelands.

Like African Americans, Native American soldiers fought on both sides of the conflict. In fact, the Revolutionary War divided and destroyed the Iroquois Confederacy. The Oneida and Tuscarora tribes sided with the Americans, while the Mohawk, Seneca, Onondaga, and Cayuga tribes sided with the British. As a result of the war, allies became enemies. No matter which side they chose, participating in the Revolutionary War did not help Native Americans to retain their lands. As the new country grew, Native Americans continued to be pushed off their lands.

The freedom and justice promised in the Declaration of Independence were noble ideals. Unfortunately, those ideals did not extend to the African Americans and Native Americans who fought so bravely for them. Today, more than 200 years later, the struggle for equality in the United States continues to be a work in progress.

Look for the reason why Native Americans fought.

> **How did their participation in the Revolutionary War affect the rights of African Americans and Native Americans? Use details from the selection and your own knowledge to support your answer.**

Trina's Answer:

Trina wrote the following answer, but it isn't effective. Her answer is problematic in several ways. Read Trina's answer below.

> African Americans and Native Americans were very brave soldiers. They fought on both sides in the American Revolution. They did not care who won. They just wanted to be free. They wanted to be left alone.

Improving Trina's Answer

Trina's answer would not get a good score. Although she stayed on topic and used supporting details from the selection, her topic does not answer the question that was asked. To improve her response, she needs to demonstrate that she understands the question. It doesn't help to stay on topic, as Trina did, if that topic is the wrong one.

Use the following questions to help you improve Trina's answer.

1. Trina needs to make sure that she answers the question asked. To focus her answer in this way, she can use the words from the question in her opening sentence.

   Rewrite Trina's opening sentence to focus the answer on the question asked. Write the new sentence here.

   _____

   _____

   _____

   _____

2. Trina needs to support her opening sentence with specific facts from the reading selection. She should explain what rights each group hoped to gain. She could say, for example, that African Americans hoped that the war would end slavery.

What could Trina say about the rights that Native Americans hoped to gain? Write the sentence here.

_____

_____

_____

3. Trina's answer needs a definite beginning, middle, and end. Now that she has an introductory paragraph, she needs to develop the body of her answer with specific details from the selection.

After her opening paragraph, Trina should write a paragraph about what happened when African Americans became soldiers. Here are an opening sentence and a closing sentence Trina could use.

_____African American soldiers fought along with white Americans in the earliest battles of the war._

_____

_____

_____

_____

_____Slavery was not abolished in the North for many decades after the war._

Complete Trina's second paragraph. On the lines above, write sentences that support the opening sentence with details from the selection.

4. Writing a separate paragraph about each group will help Trina answer the question fully.

In her next paragraph, Trina explains what happened when Native Americans became soldiers. Here are an opening sentence and a closing sentence Trina could use.

Native Americans tried to stay out of the war, but they had to fight to try to save their lands.

_____

_____

_____

_____

_____

Native Americans ended up losing most of their lands after the war.

Complete Trina's third paragraph. On the lines above, write sentences that support the opening sentence with details from the selection.

5. Conclusions are important. After restating her initial points, Trina should add a new piece of information that explains how she reached her answer.

Help Trina end her answer in a strong and interesting way. Write a closing paragraph here.

_____

_____

_____

_____

_____

_____

SCORE BUILDER

Simple things mean a lot. When you respond to an open-ended question, the way you present your answer is almost as important as the content of your answer. A sure way to get a low score is to overlook the basic conventions of standard written English. One important rule to keep in mind is subject-verb agreement. A *verb* must agree with its *subject*.

- ✓ If the subject is **singular**, the present tense of the verb ends in *s* or *es*: The settler <u>wants</u> to build on the land.

- ✓ If the subject is **plural** or if there is a **compound subject** (more than one subject), the present tense of the verb does *not* end in *s or es*: The Native Americans <u>want</u> to protect the land. The old group and the new group <u>want</u> different things.

- ✓ Be aware of the special forms of the verb *to be*:

Singular	Plural
I am	**we are**
you are	**you are**
he, she, it is	**they are**

Here are some practice sentences. Circle the correct form of the verb for each one.

1. She (be, am, is, are) the bravest woman I know.
2. Jacob and Trey (watches, watch) too much television.
3. My class always (sell, sells) more magazine subscriptions than my sister's class (do, does).

Lesson 6

Responding on Your Own

Here is a one more nonfiction reading selection. The question that follows considers the effect of modern-day reenactments of battles fought during the Revolutionary War.

Saturday Soldiers

Norberto Gomes is a pediatrician. His wife, Janet, repairs foreign cars. Their children, Zack and Clea, are middle schoolers who play soccer and love action movies. Sounds pretty normal, right? It's surprising, then, that for four or five weekends a year, the Gomes family travels back in time!

What do you learn about colonial America here?

During these weekends, Norberto shoulders a musket and teaches a unit of militiamen to march in step. Janet sets up her spinning wheel and loom. Zack carries pails of water from the river to their camp before he sneaks off to play with his friends. Clea peers into an iron kettle where a hearty stew is simmering, then adds more wood to the fire beneath it.

Norberto, Janet, Zack, and Clea belong to the Brigade of the American Revolution. Brigade members come from different backgrounds. They work all kinds of jobs. No matter where they live or what they do in their everyday lives, Brigade members have a common fascination with the Revolutionary War. They love to share their interest with others, and they do so by staging re-creations of military life in colonial America.

What historical information to you learn here?

The Brigade has about 3,000 members in more than 130 units, or local chapters. Chapters can be found in the 13 original "colonies," as well as in other states across the country, and even in Canada and Great Britain. Each chapter represents a specific military unit. Together, they include a cross-section of all of the armed forces that fought in the Revolutionary War— American rebels and Tories, British soldiers, French soldiers, Native American fighters, and German and Spanish fighters, too.

A typical Brigade weekend brings together several units. The first order of business on Friday night is to set up camp. Participants put up the tents and establish cooking and craft areas. Early on Saturday morning, drummers let the soldiers know that it is time to assemble for inspection. Another round of drumming means that it is time to practice marching and maneuvers. After more drumming, it is time for weapon practice. All of the weapons are exact copies of the muskets, rifles, cannons, bayonets, and tomahawks used in the Revolution. Later, the different units stage a mock battle. The day ends with a formal retreat ceremony, complete with musical accompaniment. On Sunday, members can attend an eighteenth-century church service. The rest of the day is similar to Saturday. The participants strike camp late on Sunday. Then they return home to their twenty-first century lives.

Historical accuracy is critically important to the Brigade. Uniforms and equipment are expected to be as authentic as the members can make them. Clothing cannot be made of synthetic materials or use zippers. Even eyeglasses have to be authentic-looking. Many members enjoy the challenge of researching and making their own clothes and equipment. They also can buy what they need from craftspeople at their encampments or from businesses that specialize in historical reproductions. When it comes to weapons, though, the Brigade has a much more modern attitude. Safety comes first, for users and bystanders.

When the Gomes family takes part in a Brigade event, it leaves the modern world behind. Norberto doesn't practice medicine. Janet doesn't fix cars. Clea and Zack don't watch movies. Instead, they live just as a soldier's family would have lived in the 1770s. From their clothes and cooking tools to their language and manners, they are colonial Americans. Thanks to the Brigade of the American Revolution, American history comes alive.

Look for historical details you would see during a reenactment.

Why are the reenactments staged by the Brigade of the American Revolution a good way to learn about history? Use details from the selection and your own ideas to support your answer.

Write your answer on the lines below.

_____

_____

_____

_____

_____

_____

_____

_____

_____

_____

_____

_____

_____

_____

_____

_____

_____

_____

_____

HINT!

When you are finished, check your answer:

✔ Have you expressed your answer clearly?

✔ Have you explored a cause-and-effect relationship in your answer?

✔ Does your answer meet the SLAMS tests?

Reader's Response!
Revise & Edit

When you have finished writing, exchange papers with a partner. As you read each other's work, answer the questions that follow.

1 Did the writer answer the question that was asked? ___ **Yes** ___ **No**

2 Did the writer use facts from the selections and his or her own ideas to support the answer? If not, what needs to be added or changed? ___ **Yes** ___ **No**

Write your response here.

_____

_____

_____

3 Was the answer clear and easy to understand? ___ **Yes** ___ **No**

4 Did the writer provide an interesting closing? ___ **Yes** ___ **No**

5 Did the writer use a variety of sentences? If not, what needs to be added or changed? ___ **Yes** ___ **No**

Write your response here.

_____

_____

_____

6 Has the writer followed all the SLAMS rules? If not, which rules were not followed? ___ **Yes** ___ **No**

Check all the boxes that apply.

S ___ L ___ A ___ M ___ S ___

7 **Give the paper back to your partner to revise and edit.**

Reviewing the Question

It's important to know how to distinguish a cause from an effect.

- A **cause** is the reason why something happens.

- An **effect** is what happens as a result of the cause. An effect may be immediate, or it may happen later. For example, in an open-ended question, you may be asked to predict an effect that might occur in the future due to a cause.

Cause-and-effect relationships can be simple or complex. In some situations, you may find that one cause leads to several effects, or that many causes come together to create one effect. When identifying cause and effect, watch for words and phrases like the following:

because   **since**   **due to**

as a result   **therefore**

These words often signal a cause-and-effect relationship.

Understanding Sequence

Your job as a reader is to recognize the correct order, or **sequence**, in which events happen. This is not always as simple as it sounds. For example, a movie may begin with a car chase that ends in an enormous crash. The movie has captured your attention. Now you want to know:

- Who are these people?
- Why were they chasing each other?

The next scene may jump back in time. The characters remember an event that has already taken place. This is called a **flashback**. It tells about something that happened before the movie began. It may provide the motivation for the car chase, or it may give an idea of who the main characters are. Sometimes scenes may also jump ahead. This kind of scene is called a **flash forward**.

Moviemakers and book authors play with time to capture interest, to explain why something happened, or to show what will happen in future. How do storytellers indicate that time has shifted? Words like *remember* or *wonder* are one way.

Leaving an extra space between paragraphs or a space with a row of dots is another way to show that something different is about to happen, as is using a different typeface—like **boldface** or *italic*.

Lesson 7

What Makes a Good Answer?

Read the first part of this story about Jamie, a boy whose family moves a lot. Then answer the question that follows to tell about sequence. Be aware of who is telling the story.

On the Move Again! —Part One

Jamie threw the calendar across his room, knocking over a juice bottle on the way. He slumped in his chair and watched the sticky liquid coat the days and weeks, while he counted: "One, two, three, four, five…"

When he reached "six," his door flew open.

"OK, Jamie. Do you want to tell me, or do you want me to guess?" Arms folded, Maria glared at him. She looked around. "Why is there juice all over the floor?" Then she spotted the calendar. She walked over and picked it up. Flipping through the dripping pages, she stopped at November 10. "Is this the problem, Jamie? Moving day?"

Jamie grunted.

"We've got three months before we move."

"Great," Jamie sulked. "Thanks for letting me know. What a relief that I have a big sister. Remind why moving again is so terrific."

"Well," Maria began, "We'll be going to a new school, a real school, not just this one-room schoolhouse in the Rockies with a bunch of computers for teachers and classmates. We'll be in a city, and there'll be lots to do and plenty of other kids."

"But I like it here. This is the best place we've ever lived. I can snowboard from October to April. Can I do that in the sunny city? No! It'll be just like the time Mom was sent to Philadelphia, only warmer. Why does she have to work for the National Park Service anyway? Why can't she… never mind." Jamie slumped again in his chair, head down, and looked at the floor.

Maria stared at her brother, considering. *Don't bug him now*, she told herself. Instead, she said, "Let me know if you want help cleaning up this mess, okay?"

Jamie nodded as his sister softly closed his door. He closed his eyes, thinking back. He couldn't help remembering what happened the last time his Mom had been assigned to a big city….

Pay attention to the date in this paragraph.

In which month does the story take place?

• •

Jamie opened the door and walked into Room 234, pass in one hand, information card in the other. The teacher took the card, read it quickly, then smiled at him. Meanwhile, Jamie felt all eyes on him, checking him out. Right now they were focused on his clothes—plaid shirt, hiking boots, skinny-leg new jeans. He was already down for the count. Everyone else was straight out of MTV land.

"Class, this is your new classmate, Jamie Mendez. He's from..." The teacher hesitated. "Is this correct, Jamie? You're from Olympic National Forest?"

Jamie wanted to kick himself. Why did he write that? As he walked to his seat, he heard the whispers: "Tarzan." "George of the Jungle." "Tree-hugger." School went from bad to worse. The school was so big it took months for Jamie to break through and make friends. Even when he did, then what? He'd probably have to move again.

Why is this text in italics?

A writer may change the order of story events, or the sequence. How does the sequence change in this story? How do you know? What does it tell you about the character or the plot?

Carla's Answer:

Carla wrote a successful answer to this question. Read what she wrote, then answer the questions that follow. They will help you understand what makes her answer so successful.

In this story, the author changes the *sequence* by going back in time. This technique is called the *flashback technique*. This technique helps the reader understand why Jamie is so upset about moving again.

The scene opens with Jamie throwing a calendar across the room. We don't know why it happens, but we know he's mad. When we read "He couldn't help remembering," we're pretty sure that the story will go back in time. There is also a pause at the end of that sentence, shown by (...), and there is an extra space between paragraphs. Finally, the "remembering" section, or flashback, is in italics.

In the flashback, we learn about Jamie's past experience. He remembers how awful it was to go to a new school the last time they moved to a big city. He felt like all the kids laughed at him *because of his clothes and because of where he used to live.* This flashback helps us understand why he feels upset now.

Carla's answer has all the elements that test scorers like to see.

✓ She sums up the main part of the answer in the opening sentence.

✓ She tells what clues the author gives to alert the reader that a flashback is coming.

✓ She gives details from the story to support her answer.

✓ She writes clear, interesting sentences.

What Makes Carla's Answer Successful?

Now let's take a closer look at Carla's answer to see why it works.

1. In her first paragraph, Carla writes a sentence that tells her main idea.

   What is Carla's main-idea sentence? Write Carla's sentence here.

   _____

   _____

2. In her first paragraph, Carla demonstrates that she understands the author's sequencing technique.

   In which sentence does she explain the technique? Write Carla's sentence here.

   _____

   _____

3. Carla organizes her answer into three paragraphs.

   a. **What is the main idea of the first paragraph? Write your answer here.**

   _____

   _____

   b. **What is the main idea of the second paragraph? Write your answer here.**

   _____

   _____

   _____

   c. **What is the main idea of the third paragraph? Write your answer here.**

   _____

   _____

   _____

4. Carla describes four ways that the author alerts the reader that a flashback is coming. One way is that she recalls the text from the story, "He couldn't help remembering."

   Find three other ways of indicating a flashback that Carla mentions. Write Carla's sentences here.

   _____

   _____

   _____

   _____

5. Carla explains what the author wanted the reader to learn from the flashback. Here is one sentence with details: "He remembers how awful it was to go to a new school the last time they moved to a big city."

   Find another sentence in which Carla provides details from the flashback. Write Carla's sentence here.

   _____

   _____

   _____

   _____

6. Carla makes her sentences interesting by combining ideas into longer, more complex sentences. Here is one example: "When we read 'He couldn't help remembering,' we're pretty sure that the story will go back in time."

   Find another sentence in which Carla combines ideas. Write the sentence here.

   _____

   _____

   _____

Tools & Tips

When you first learned to read, you learned to recognize some **Reading Road Signs**. For example, you learned that a group of words was a sentence because it began with a capital letter and ended with a period, a question mark, or an exclamation point. You learned to recognize the punctuation marks that alert the reader when someone is about to speak.

When you read this story, you learned how a writer can show a change in sequence through punctuation, vocabulary, and design or format.

1. Review the first part of the story (pp. 58–59). Which Reading Road Signs alert you to a flashback?
   Write them here.

   _____

   _____

   _____

2. Look at the next part of the story (pp. 64–65), and find the Reading Road Signs.
   Write them here and tell what they show.

   _____

   _____

   _____

   _____

3. Turn to the last part of the story (p. 70), and find the Reading Road Signs.
   Write them here and tell what they show.

   _____

   _____

   _____

Lesson 8

Revising and Improving a Weak Answer

Read the second part of the story about Jamie. Then answer the question that follows about sequence. Be aware of who is telling the story.

On the Move Again! —Part Two

Does this action take place before or after the previous story?

That night at dinner, Maria noticed that Jamie didn't say much. He moved his food around his plate a few times, then he stopped.

His mother looked at him and raised one eyebrow. "Jamie, are you okay? Is there something you want to talk about?"

"No."

"Is it about moving?"

Maria chimed in. "I think it is Mom. This afternoon, we…"

Jamie looked at his sister sharply, put down his napkin, and mumbled, "Excuse me." He stood up, then stomped off to his room and slammed the door.

"There'll be no slamming doors in this house!" his mom called after him. The door to Jamie's room opened, then closed again quietly.

"He's taking it really hard, isn't he?" Juanita Mendez asked Maria.

"He likes it here. A lot."

"How about you?" Juanita asked.

"Oh, I'm okay with moving."

Juanita nodded, then looked at her watch. "I hate to leave you in charge again, but I have to start interviewing new people for my job."

"You go, Mom, I'll clean up."

"Aren't you online with your computer study group tonight?"

"Doing the dishes doesn't take that long. Besides, I'm running the group tonight."

Look for Reading Road Signs that tell you about a change in sequence.

After clearing the table, Maria turned on the water. It ran hot for a few seconds, then turned cold, and stopped completely. "Living here is like camping out all the time," she muttered to herself.

By the time she pumped more water and heated it on the wood stove, her mind was elsewhere. She knew exactly what it was going to be like three months from now…

Maria slung her new backpack over her shoulder, took one final look in the hall mirror, and walked out the door onto the city street. She had been here for two weeks, but she still felt a thrill as her foot touched pavement. In five minutes she saw more buildings and more people than she had in a whole month in the mountains.

At her new school, she met Mr. Sudbury, the guidance counselor. By 10 o'clock everything was in place. Mr. Sudbury took her to her computer class and introduced her to the teacher. Ms. Sweeney set her up at a computer right away and handed her a list of group assignments to pick from.

Maria turned to the girl next to her. "Hi, I'm Maria. Which group are you working with?"

"I'm Shaniqua, and I'm with the women's basketball data team. We keep track of every play and try to figure out which plays work best for us."

"I love basketball, but I'd never make the school team."

"You can still work with us."

Maria smiled. A real project, a friend, and her favorite sport—all in one. She loved the city!

> What do the italics tell you?

> **A writer may change the order of story events, or the sequence. How does the sequence change in this story? How do you know? What does it tell you about the character or the plot?**

Justin's Answer:

Justin wrote the following answer to the question. Unfortunately, it is not an answer that would get a good score. Read his answer below.

> First, Jamie slams the door. He's unhappy. His mom leaves for work. Maria does the dishes. When her mom leaves for work. There's no hot water so she has to heat some up. She hates where they live. Then she goes to a new school in the big city. She likes walking in the city because there are lots of people. She makes friends right away. And gets to work for the basketball team.

Improving Justin's Answer

Justin's answer has a lot of details. His details are written in the right order, too. Even so, Justin's answer would not receive a high score.

✓ Justin doesn't show evidence that he understands that the author is using a flash forward.

✓ As a result, it sounds like Justin thinks that author is telling about Maria's first day in her new school, not a first day that Maria imagines she might have in the future.

✓ Justin doesn't explain or elaborate any of the details in his answer.

✓ Some of Justin's sentences are fragments.

✓ Justin interprets a character's actions only once.

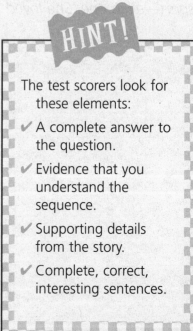

HINT!

The test scorers look for these elements:

✔ A complete answer to the question.

✔ Evidence that you understand the sequence.

✔ Supporting details from the story.

✔ Complete, correct, interesting sentences.

Use the questions below to help you revise Justin's answer and turn it into a successful one.

1. Justin needs an opening sentence that tells the reader the main idea of his answer.
   What would be a good opening sentence for this question? Write the sentence here.

   _____

   _____

   _____

   _____

2. Justin's answer should next include some details from the story to explain how the story begins. Justin has already provided some details, but they are not very well thought out.
   Write at least two new sentences for Justin that establish the beginning of the story.

   _____

   _____

   _____

   _____

   _____

   _____

3. Justin needs to explain how the author lets the readers know that the next scene is a flash forward.
   How can Justin explain the author's flash-forward techniques? Write about the details from the story that show these flash-forward techniques.

   _____

   _____

   _____

   _____

   _____

4. Justin's answer should include details to show what the author wants the reader to learn from the flash forward. Here is one detail that he provides: "She likes walking in the city because there are lots of people there."

Find additional details from the selection that he can use. Write at least two new sentences for Justin here.

_____

_____

_____

_____

_____

5. Justin needs to correct the sentence fragments in his answer. Read this sentence fragment: "When her Mom leaves for work."

a. **Correct the fragment by joining it to the sentence that comes before it. Write the corrected sentence here.**

_____

_____

_____

b. **Find another fragment in Justin's answer. Write it here.**

_____

_____

c. **Correct the fragment by joining it to the sentence that comes before it. Write the corrected sentence here.**

_____

_____

_____

SCORE BUILDER

Verbs change to show time. Make sure you write verbs correctly.

✓ Some verbs are **regular verbs** because they all change the same way to show the *past tense*. Once you learn the rule on how to make the verb past tense, you can apply the rule to all the regular verbs.

✓ Some verbs are **irregular verbs**. To show past tense, these verbs change in different ways. The only way to learn the past tense of irregular verbs is through repetition. You can create repetition by using them often, such as saying them out loud, spelling them, writing them, and so on. If you practice them often, you'll find them easy to remember.

Here are some irregular verbs. Fill in the past tense to complete the chart.

Present Tense	Past Tense
throw	threw
give	gave
fly	flew
take	took
write	wrote
say	_____
leave	_____
is	_____
see	_____
wake	_____

Lesson 9

Responding on Your Own

On the Move Again! –Part Three

Juanita Mendez sipped her tea, enjoying the ten-minute break in the meeting. People were eating, talking, laughing, sometimes all at once. Juanita realized once again why she loved what she did. These people were the faces of America—its native origins, its European past, its present and future newcomers from all over the globe.

She had been in the Park Service for almost 20 years now. The first ten years were with her husband Carlos. Then he had died on a rescue mission, and the last ten years she had been a single mother with two children. Now she wondered if it was time to give it up. She remembered what it was like the first few years alone with the children…

> Look for a word that tells you if this is a flashback or a flash forward.

• •

The cabin pressure changed in the airplane, and both kids woke up. Maria was bright-eyed and ready for landing. Jamie, as usual, took a long time waking. Transitions were always difficult for him—getting up, going to bed, going to school, coming home. Maria was just the opposite. She liked change.

Three weeks later, Juanita received two calls from the school. The first call was from Maria's teacher. She was concerned that Maria couldn't settle down. She whizzed through the day, doing some reading, some writing, some math, and never finishing anything. The second call was from Jamie's teacher. Jamie couldn't seem to get moving. Once he started on something, he could stay with it for half the morning, but he had trouble getting started. He was reluctant to change colors when painting. He had only one friend.

• •

That night Juanita called a family meeting. She told Jamie and Maria about her memory. "Why am I telling you this? I think that wherever you are or wherever you go, your personalities stay the same. Since you'll both be in the same school, I'm asking you to each do a job. Maria, your job is to find out everything new about the school to share with Jamie. Jamie, you'll find out which classes will help you both continue the programs you already like." Juanita took a deep breath. "And my job will be to spend part of the time planning our next step. Maybe we'll stay in one place for a while, or maybe we'll move on, but this time it will be a family decision. What do you think?"

Their smiles were her answer.

> Why does the story go back to regular type here?

A writer may change the order of story events, or the sequence. How does the sequence change in this part of the story? How do you know? What does it tell you about the character or the plot?

Write your answer on the lines below.

_____

_____

_____

_____

_____

_____

_____

_____

_____

_____

_____

_____

_____

_____

_____

_____

_____

_____

HINT!

When you are finished, check your answer.

✔ Have you identified the sequence change in the story?

✔ Have you supported your answer with details from the selection?

✔ Does your answer meet all the SLAMS tests?

Reader's Response
Revise & Edit

When you have finished writing, exchange papers with a partner. As you read each other's answers, follow these steps:

1 Did the writer answer the question completely? ___ **Yes** ___ **No**
If not, what needs to be added or changed?

Write your response here.

_____

_____

_____

2 Did the writer identify the correct sequence change?

3 Did the writer explain how the sequence change was indicated? ___ **Yes** ___ **No**
If not, what needs to be added or changed?

Write your response here.

_____

_____

_____

4 Did the writer describe what the time change ___ **Yes** ___ **No**
told the reader about the characters or the plot?
If not, what needs to be added or changed?

Write your response here.

_____

_____

_____

5 Has the writer followed all the SLAMS rules? ___ **Yes** ___ **No**
If not, which rules were not followed?

Check all the boxes that apply.

S ___   L ___   A ___   M ___   S ___

6 **Give the paper back to your partner to revise and edit.**

Reviewing the Question

Questions about *sequence* usually ask you to notice if all the steps are in the right order. They might also ask you to make a list of the steps or the action in the selection, in order. They might even ask you to supply missing steps. This unit asks a different question. It asks you to apply your knowledge of how authors *indicate a change* in sequence.

- Changing the sequence, or shifting time, can mean telling about an event that took place before the main part of the story. This change is called a **flashback**.

- Shifting time can also mean letting the reader know what could happen or what a character imagines might happen in the future. A scene that takes place in the future is called a **flash forward**.

The important thing to remember is that authors shift time for a reason. They use these devices—flashbacks and flash forwards—to tell the reader more about a character or to reveal more about the plot. Recognizing this technique will help you answer questions about sequence.

Read the selection on these pages. Then answer the questions on pages 76–78.

Eggs in Blue Water

"We're ready for the second step of our experiment," Ms. Graff told her science class. She set down a container that held two eggs floating in a liquid.

"Wow!" exclaimed Kerry. "The eggs don't have shells anymore."

"They must have shells," Clark insisted. "The shells couldn't just disappear."

"Maybe Ms. Graff took the shells off when we weren't here," said Selena.

"Think!" Ms. Graff reminded them. "What was in the container with the eggs?"

"Oh, I remember," said Selena. "We put the eggs in vinegar. You mean the vinegar dissolved the shells?"

"Then what's that around them?" demanded Clark. "I thought that was the shells."

"It's the membrane!" said Kerry. "Right?"

"Exactly," said Ms. Graff. She took out two empty containers. "Now we're going to continue our experiment, using these same eggs."

She filled one container with 150 milliliters of water and a few drops of blue food coloring. In the other container, she poured 150 milliliters of corn syrup. Using a special device, she weighed each egg and asked Kerry to record their weights. Then she asked Clark to gently place one egg into the container of blue-colored water, and she asked Selena to gently place the other egg into the container of corn syrup.

"That's it for now," Ms. Graff said. "Let's put the eggs back in the refrigerator for another 24 hours. What do you think we'll find when we take the containers out tomorrow?"

Clark answered right away. "There won't be any eggs left. They'll have dissolved completely."

"I don't think they will have changed at all," said Selena. "The membranes will keep them safe."

The next day, the class could hardly wait to see what had happened.

"Okay, Clark," said Ms. Graff. "Come over here and check the weight of the egg that's been in the blue water. Do it carefully because it does still have its membrane."

"Look at that," said Clark. "It's gotten heavier. Some of the blue water must have gone through the membrane and into the egg."

"That's a good guess," said Ms. Graff. "Here's a way to make sure. We recorded how much blue water was in the container before—right? Its volume was 150 milliliters. Look at the container. How much water is in there now?"

"The amount of water has gone down," said Selena and Kerry together. "Let's see what happened to the other egg."

They checked the egg and found that its weight had decreased, then they checked the corn syrup and found that its volume had increased.

"That's not possible," Clark announced. "If the blue water could get into the egg, the corn syrup should have, too. It's a liquid. It could go right through that membrane, just like water."

"Well, I guess something did go through the membrane," countered Selena, "only it went the other way. Some of the egg ended up going through the membrane and into the corn syrup. That's why the egg weighs less than it did before, and why the volume of the corn syrup is higher."

"That's right," Ms. Graff confirmed. "From our first experiment, we learned that water will always move from an area of high concentration to an area of lower concentration. Now we've introduced some new elements. First, there's the egg's membrane, which will let water molecules go through, but larger molecules can't pass through the tiny spaces in the membrane. Then, one of the eggs is in corn syrup, which contains a little water. Most of the corn syrup is not water: Its molecules are larger than water molecules. That means there is less water outside the egg than inside it. So who can describe what happened?"

1 Fact and Opinion

The students in Ms. Graff's class express their opinions and make statements of fact during the science experiment. What are some of their opinions? What are some of their facts?

_____

_____

_____

_____

_____

_____

_____

_____

_____

_____

_____

_____

_____

_____

_____

_____

_____

_____

_____

_____

_____

_____

2 Cause and Effect ....

Explain the science experiment. What did the students do? What were the results?

_____

_____

_____

_____

_____

_____

_____

_____

_____

_____

_____

_____

_____

_____

_____

_____

_____

_____

_____

_____

_____

_____

3 Understanding Sequence

Imagine that you want to tell your class how to do the experiment that Ms. Graff's class did. Describe what materials your classmates would need and what steps they would need to follow. Make sure you write the steps in correct sequence.

_____

_____

_____

_____

_____

_____

_____

_____

_____

_____

_____

_____

_____

_____

_____

_____

_____

_____

_____

_____

_____

_____

_____

Part B

Writing Extended Answers

Reading What Is on the Page

When you read for specific information, you are reading what is on the page. Some open-ended questions ask you for specific information from a reading selection. When you answer this kind of question, you can find everything you need for your answer in the selection itself. You don't need to tell about your own experience or to draw conclusions about what you have read.

When reading what is on the page, you may be asked to do one of the following:

- Find the main idea and supporting details.
- Summarize the selection.
- Tell about a particular person, place, or event.
- Compare two people, places, or events.

Your job as a **reader** is to identify the relevant information in the reading selection. Your job as a **writer** is to organize that information to answer the question completely.

Lesson 10

What Makes a Good Answer?

The following selection includes both facts and opinions. The question that follows will ask you to find the facts.

Elephant Talk

Katy Payne stands in the dark in the middle of a Kenyan wildlife preserve. She listens intently. The moon sheds a gentle light across a clearing, and Katy can just see the shapes of dozens of large creatures emerging from the forest.

They are elephants. They begin making noises—rumbles and screams, trumpets and growls. As a scientist who's been studying elephants for many years, Katy Payne understands much of what the elephants "say." She hears lost elephant calves calling for their mothers and male elephants challenging each other. Even though Payne listens closely, she knows she's not hearing everything. Another level of communication is going on, one that humans can't hear.

In 1984, Katy Payne was visiting a zoo in Oregon. While near the elephant enclosure, she felt at certain times a throbbing in the air around the elephants. It reminded her of a car traveling at high speed with the window open, or of standing next to an organ playing very low notes. Payne had been studying the songs of whales. She suddenly wondered whether elephants might have a song of their own. She returned to the zoo with a tape recorder and recorded the vibrations at low speed. Listening to the recordings, Payne realized that she had discovered a new system of communication. Elephants were using **infrasound** to communicate with each other.

Katy Payne couldn't wait to find out what her discovery meant. She traveled to Amboseli National Park in Kenya, Africa, and began to study the elephants there. Scientists had already observed the many forms of elephant communication they could see and hear. They had also drawn conclusions about what some of the behaviors meant. For example, the trumpeting noise that many people associate with elephants shows excitement, fear, or aggression. Mothers calm their calves with soft rumbles, or they slap them with their trunks for discipline. Two elephants might entwine their trunks together as a greeting. Many other behaviors puzzled the scientists. Could infrasound be the key to understanding them?

You can find sounds elephants make here.

Explanations of sounds are found here.

Infrasound did unlock at least one puzzle. Elephants had always seemed able to communicate over very long distances, but no one could figure out how. Scientists now realized that the elephants were able to pick up faraway infrasound signals that the scientists couldn't hear.

No one is quite sure how elephants create or hear infrasound. One scientist has suggested that elephants feel infrasound through their feet. He says that the elephants seem to lean forward and pay attention to the ground, as if they can feel the low rumbles coming from other elephants.

To solve these mysteries, Katy Payne founded the Elephant Listening Project (ELP) in 1999. Scientists participating in the ELP have come to Amboseli State Park to set up audio recorders. Katy Payne and her colleagues have learned that elephants can hear and respond to infrasound calls over distances as great as five miles. Elephants also recognize which calls come from elephants in their own family or herd.

Although the scientists are not sure what each and every call means, they have identified over thirty different calls. They think the calls can be used, among other things, to signal danger, to give directions as the elephants migrate, and to find mates. The calls are especially important for mothers looking after their calves. Also, only females stay together in herds, so infrasound helps the loner males talk to them over long distances.

Katy Payne followed a hunch that has opened a whole new world of mammal communication. Following her lead, scientists have now discovered that giraffes, hippos, rhinoceroses, and cassowaries (flightless birds from New Guinea) use infrasound communication, too. Her discovery serves as a reminder of how little people know about the natural world. Scientists like Katy Payne open new worlds to us. They show us that animals communicate and live in ways that we are only just beginning to understand.

More sounds explained here!

Read the open-ended question below about the selection you have just read. Notice that it asks you about what is on the page. You need to find information in the selection.

> **What are some methods elephants use to communicate? Use details from the selection in your answer.**

Jayna's Answer:

Here is Jayna's answer. Read what she wrote. Then answer the questions that follow to see why her response is successful.

Elephants have many different ways of communicating with each other. Some you can see, some you can hear, and some are impossible for humans to understand.

Elephants communicate through noises and gestures. If you were watching a group of elephants, you might hear them trumpet to show fear or make rumbling noises to calm their babies. You might see a mom elephant slapping her baby with her trunk as punishment. They also might make screaming or growling sounds. You might see them twist their trunks together to say "hi." These are things you can see and hear when you watch elephants.

Elephants also have another level of communication. Some sounds are called infrasound. They are below the level of what people can hear. These sounds feel the way the air does when you're going fast in a car with the window open or standing next to an organ that is playing low. Elephants may feel these vibrations through their feet. They can use infrasound over long distances to communicate. They can use it close up, too, and they can tell if it is their friends or relatives talking. Elephants communicate in many ways, and today scientists study elephants to learn more about what they are saying.

What Makes Jayna's Answer Work?

Jayna's answer has all the elements the test scorers look for:

✓ She states her main idea clearly.

✓ She uses details from the selection to back up her main idea.

✓ She organizes her answer in paragraphs.

✓ She has a clear closing.

✓ She writes in clear, complete sentences.

Now let's take a closer look at Jayna's answer to see what makes it successful.

1. Jayna begins by stating her main idea.

   What is Jayna's main idea? Write the sentences that states her main idea here.

   _____

   _____

   _____

   _____

2. Jayna mentions elephant communication that people can see.

   What details from the selection does she include? Write Jayna's sentence here.

   _____

   _____

   _____

3. Jayna also discusses elephant communication that people can hear.

   What details from the selection does she include? Write Jayna's sentences here.

   _____

   _____

   _____

4. Jayna writes about another kind of elephant communication in her third paragraph.

How does she introduce this paragraph? Write Jayna's sentence here.

_____

_____

_____

5. Jayna provides details and examples to develop her third paragraph.

What details from the story does she add to support her first sentence? Write two of Jayna's sentences here.

_____

_____

_____

_____

_____

6. Jayna finishes her essay by summing up her answer.

What is Jayna's conclusion? Write Jayna's closing sentence here.

_____

_____

_____

Tools & Tips

This reading selection introduces a new word: *infrasound*. You learned that this word means sounds that humans can't hear. The prefix *infra-* comes from Latin and means "beneath" or "below." An infrasound, therefore, is a sound below the range that humans can hear.

What do you think *infrared* means?

Write your answer here.

_____

_____

Many English words have parts that come from the Latin or Greek languages. Read the words on this list. Underline the parts that are the same.

aspire	expire	respire
conspire	inspire	transpire

The root *-spire* comes from the Latin word *spirare*, which means "to breathe." By understanding the prefixes attached to *spire*, you can figure out the words' meanings. Here are the meanings of the prefixes.

Prefix	Meaning
a-	at, toward
ex-	out
re-	back, again
con-	together
in-	into
trans-	across, over

Think about what each word in the first list means. Discuss your ideas with a partner. Then look up the definitions to see how close your definitions were.

Lesson 11

Strategy: Find Information in the Text

When you are writing to explain something that you have read, you need to include specific information from the reading selection. Questions that ask you to explain "what is on the page" usually begin with question words like *who, what, when, and where*. The information you need, then, is usually about someone, something, some time, or some place. While you read, keep these questions in mind and look for words or groups of words that answer them. When you start to write your answer, you will have a good idea of where to find the information you need.

A. Try it with these questions. Read each sentence from the reading selection and think about what question it answers. Then read the three questions that follow and decide which one you could answer with the information from the selection sentence. Put a check mark next to that question.

1. As a scientist who's been studying elephants for many years, Katy Payne understands much of what the elephants "say."

   ☐ a. Who is Katy Payne?

   ☐ b. When did Katy Payne study elephants?

   ☐ c. Where did Katy Payne study elephants?

2. To solve these mysteries, Katy Payne founded the Elephant Listening Project (ELP) in 1999.

   ☐ a. Where is the Elephant Listening Project located?

   ☐ b. What is infrasound?

   ☐ c. When did Katy Payne found the Elephant Listening Project?

3. She returned to the zoo with a tape recorder and recorded the vibrations at low speed. Listening to the recordings, Payne realized that she had discovered a new system of communication.

   ☐ a. What did Katy Payne discover about the recorded vibrations?

   ☐ b. When was Katy Payne interested in elephant communication?

   ☐ c. Who is Payne?

4. It reminded her of a car traveling at high speed with the window open, or of standing next to an organ playing very low notes.

   ☐ a. What did Katy Payne discover about elephants?

   ☐ b. When did Katy Payne think elephants could communicate infrasonically?

   ☐ c. What does Katy Payne compare to the feeling of infrasound for humans?

B. Here are more sentences from the reading selection, followed by questions. Which group of words in the sentence answers the question? Write the words on the lines. Do not write the whole sentence. Use only the words that answer the question.

1. Katy Payne and her colleagues have learned that elephants can hear and respond to infrasound calls over distances as great as five miles.

   What have scientists learned about elephant communication?

   _____

   _____

2. One scientist has suggested that elephants can feel infrasound through their feet. He says that the elephants seem to lean forward and pay attention to the ground, as if they can feel the low rumbles coming from other elephants through their feet.

   What does one scientist suggest about how elephants "hear" infrasound?

   _____

   _____

3. In 1984, Katy Payne was visiting a zoo in Oregon. While near the elephant enclosure, she felt at certain times a throbbing in the air around the elephants.

   When did Katy Payne discover elephant infrasound?

   _____

   _____

4. Katy Payne stands in the dark in the middle of a Kenyan wildlife preserve.

   Where is Katy Payne?

   _____

   _____

5. Mothers calm their calves with soft rumbles, or they slap them with their trunks for discipline.

   What do mother elephants do to discipline their calves?

   _____

   _____

Lesson 12

Strategy: Keep to One Main Idea in a Paragraph

Sometimes, when you have a lot to say, you might write too much for one paragraph. Read the example below. As you read, try to identify the main idea.

If you were a scientist watching elephants on the savanna, you would be able to see many different elephant interactions. For instance, older calves might be fanning their ears, lounging around, and chewing grass. They might start to play by gently sniffing each other with their trunks. You could watch as the matriarch, or female in charge, calls the herd to the feeding ground. She might be followed by more adult females and young calves. It might be a surprise to you that elephants are led by matriarchs. A matriarch is a wise and experienced mother who leads the herd. The male elephants are loners. They leave the herd when they are old enough to live on their own.

Can you identify the main idea? It's difficult! One of the reasons why this paragraph is so long is because it has two main ideas. This paragraph should really be two paragraphs.

A. Answer the questions below, based on the above paragraph.

1. **Read the sentences below. Which sentence best expresses the first main idea?**

_____ a. Scientists watching elephants in the field are able to observe many different behaviors.

_____ b. Watching elephants on the savanna, you might get a chance to see calves playing.

2. **Read these sentences. Which sentence best expresses the second main idea?**

_____ a. Male elephants do not live with the herd.

_____ b. Elephants are led by wise female leaders.

3. Reread the above paragraph. Where do you think the writer should break the paragraph into two paragraphs?

Write the first sentence of the second paragraph below.

_____

_____

_____

B. Read this paragraph about giraffes. Then answer the questions that follow to revise and improve it.

Giraffes are the tallest land animals. The tallest giraffe on record lived in a London zoo and was twenty feet tall. Even smaller giraffes have incredibly long necks (up to six feet in length) that weigh nearly six hundred pounds. Most adult giraffes could look straight into a second-story window. Because of their height, giraffes are browsers that eat tree leaves high off the ground. They can reach many sources of food that are too high for other animals. Their favorite food is the acacia tree, which has sharp thorns, but their thick black tongues aren't affected by the thorns.

1. Which sentence expresses the first main idea?
   Write it here.

   _____

   _____

   _____

2. Which sentence expresses the second main idea?
   Write it here.

   _____

   _____

   _____

3. Which sentence should begin a new paragraph?
   Write it here.

   _____

   _____

   _____

> ## HINT!
> When you write, make sure each paragraph has just one main idea. If a paragraph is much longer than the rest, check it carefully. You might have introduced a second main idea.

Lesson 13

Strategy: Write a Good Closing

One of the elements that made Jayna's response successful was her closing sentence. She didn't end her answer after she had provided two sets of details about elephant communication. Instead, she summed up her response.

Jayna's Closing:

> Elephants communicate in many ways, and today scientists study elephants to learn more about what they are saying.

Jayna followed another important strategy, too. She connected her closing sentence to her opening sentences without repeating the opening:

Jayna's Opening:

> Elephants have many different ways of communicating with each other. Some you can see, some you can hear, and some are impossible for humans to understand.

A. Take a closer look at Jayna's answer.

   1. One idea in Jayna's opening is also in her closing. Which idea is it?

   Write your answer here.

   _____

   2. One idea in Jayna's closing is new. Which idea is it?

   Write your answer here.

   _____

B. **Try it. There is more than one way to end Jayna's answer. Reread her answer on page 84 and think about her opening. Then write two more ways she could close her answer. You can write one sentence or two for each closing.**

   _____

   _____

   _____

   _____

   _____

   _____

Exchange your closings with a partner and talk about them. Which ones work best? Why?

Miles read the same selection as Jayna, but he answered a different open-ended question. Here's the question that Miles answered:

How did Katy Payne get involved in studying the way elephants communicate?

Read Miles's answer. His opening sentence is in bold.

Miles's Answer:

Katy Payne started studying the way elephants communicate almost by accident. She knew something about animal communication because she had been studying the way whales communicate, using low sounds. One day at the zoo, however, she suddenly felt something strange near the elephant enclosure. There was a vibration in the air. She brought a tape recorder to the zoo and recorded the vibrations at low speed. Katy Payne was pretty sure she had discovered an infrasound communication system.

Scientists already knew a lot about the elephant communication they could hear and see. They knew what many sounds and gestures meant. They also knew that elephants seemed to be able to communicate even when they were far apart. Katy's idea that they used infrasound communication interested other scientists. Katy set up the Elephant Listening Project in Africa to record and study the sounds elephants make.

4. Miles's answer doesn't have a closing sentence. Write a closing for his answer.

Write your closing here.

_____

_____

_____

_____

HINT!

Try to connect the closing sentence to the opening sentence without repeating the opening one exactly.

Lesson 14

Revising and Improving a Weak Answer

The next step in learning how to write a successful answer is to try to improve an answer that is incomplete or unsuccessful. Reread the reading selection *Elephant Talk* on pages 82 and 83.

How did Katy Payne discover that elephants used infrasound communication?

Shawn's Answer:

Shawn tried to answer this question, but his response is weak. Look at what he wrote. Then think about what you have learned in this unit about writing a good answer. You will also use the questions that follow to help you revise and improve Shawn's answer.

> Katy Payne discovered elephants could use infrasound at a zoo. She had studied other animals and she was pretty smart. She noticed something weird was going on. She investigated it. It turned out the elephants could communicate through infrasound.

Improving Shawn's Answer

Shawn has started to answer the question:

✓ He mentions that Katy Payne discovered elephant infrasound while at a zoo.

✓ He mentions that she had been studying animal communication.

However, Shawn's answer is very short. He has not included any details from the selection. Someone who had not read the selection would not be able to understand how Katy Payne discovered elephant infrasound after reading Shawn's answer. The test scorers would probably agree that Shawn's answer is not a successful one.

Help Shawn revise his answer so it would get a better score. Answer these questions to help you fill in what Shawn left out.

1. Does Shawn state the main idea? Is his first sentence the main idea or a supporting detail?

   What do we learn about Katy Payne that could form a main-idea sentence? For example, what qualities or skills helped Katy make her discovery? Write a new opening sentence here.

   _____

   _____

   _____

2. What else would be helpful to know about Katy? What details could Shawn add after his second sentence: "She had studied other animals and she was pretty smart"?

   Write the new sentence or sentences here.

   _____

   _____

   _____

   _____

3. Shawn has told us that Katy "noticed something weird was going on."

   What details could he add after this sentence? Write the new sentence or sentences here.

   _____

   _____

   _____

   _____

4. Shawn also says, "She investigated it," but he doesn't provide any details.

   How did Katy investigate? Write the new sentence or sentences here.

   _____

   _____

   _____

   _____

5. Shawn's last sentence probably now needs to be revised.

   What details could you add to make Shawn's last sentence fit the new information you've added? Write a new sentence or sentences here.

   _____

   _____

   _____

   _____

   _____

6. Shawn needs a strong closing sentence to go with his new opening.

   What generalization or interesting statement could Shawn make about how Katy Payne discovered elephant infrasound? Write the new sentence or sentences here.

   _____

   _____

   _____

   _____

   _____

SCORE BUILDER

How's your spelling? Spelling rules can be complicated! Two things are true about the spelling rules of English words:

- The English language has more sounds than letters in the alphabet. This means one spelling can stand for several different sounds.

- Also, the same sound can be spelled in different ways. Different combinations of letters may be pronounced the same way.

1. Say these words out loud. Which of the statements above do these words illustrate?

feet   treat

Pete   piece

2. Say these words out loud. Which of the statements above do these words illustrate?

thought   about

tour   rough

As you read, pay attention to words that have the same letters, but different sounds; or the same sounds, but different spellings. The more familiar with and aware of these words you become, the more easily you'll be able to recognize their spellings in the future.

98

Lesson 15

Responding on Your Own

Here is a final question about *Elephant Talk*. You will write this answer on your own. As you plan and write your answer, think about what you have learned from analyzing Jayna's answer and improving Shawn's answer. Also, use the following to help write your response:

✓ the **strategies** you practiced

✓ the tips you were given in **Tools & Tips**

✓ the reminders in the **Score Builder**

Read this question. The information you need is in the reading selection.

> **It has been more than two decades since Katy Payne first discovered elephant infrasound. What have scientists learned since then about elephant infrasound communication? What are they still exploring? Use details from the selection in your response.**

Write your answer here.

_____

_____

_____

_____

_____

_____

_____

_____

_____

_____

_____

_____

_____

_____

HINT!

Ask yourself these questions:

✓ Have I stated the main idea in the opening?

✓ Have I organized my response into paragraphs, each with its own main idea and supporting details?

✓ Have I written a clear closing?

✓ Have I written clear, complete, and interesting sentences?

Reader's Response
Revise & Edit

When you have finished writing, exchange papers with a partner. As you read each other's answers, follow these steps:

1 Is the main idea clearly stated in the opening?   ___ **Yes** ___ **No**
If not what needs to be added?
Write your response here.

_____

_____

_____

2 Did the writer organize the response into paragraphs?   ___ **Yes** ___ **No**

3 Did the writer provide enough details from the   ___ **Yes** ___ **No**
selection to support each main idea?
If not, what needs to be added?
Write your response here.

_____

_____

_____

4 Does the closing connect ideas to the opening   ___ **Yes** ___ **No**

5 Are the writer's sentences correct and interesting?   ___ **Yes** ___ **No**

6 Has the writer followed all the SLAMS rules?   ___ **Yes** ___ **No**
If not, which rules were not followed?
Check all the boxes that apply.

S ___   L ___   A ___   M ___   S ___

7 **Give the paper back to your partner to revise and edit.**

Reviewing the Question

Many open-ended questions ask you to read what is on the page. Remember that questions like these don't ask you to draw your own conclusions about what you've read nor to tell about your own experience. Instead, they ask you to provide information from the reading selection. Here are some examples of open-ended questions that ask you to tell about what is on the page:

- What, in general, is this selection about?

- Who is Katy Payne? What does she do?

- Where does Katy Payne mostly study elephants?

- What techniques do elephants use to communicate?

- When did Katy Payne develop her theory?

- What is the purpose of the Elephant Listening Project?

Reading Between the Lines

Good readers remember and understand the information in a selection, but that's only part of the job. Good readers also know how to **read between the lines**. Reading between the lines means recognizing ideas that are not stated directly. It means *making inferences* or *drawing conclusions* about what you have read. Open-ended questions often ask you to read between the lines. Instead of asking you what happened in a selection, for example, an open-ended question might ask you to explain why or how something happened.

In fact, questions that ask you to read between the lines often have the word *why* in them. Open-ended questions like these might ask you to:

- explain actions or events;

- explain what a person is like based on what he or she does or says;

- guess what has just happened in a story or predict what might happen next.

In this unit, you will practice answering open-ended questions that ask you to read between the lines. You will answer questions about ideas that are implied in the selection but that are not actually stated on the page.

Lesson 16

What Makes a Good Answer?

Read the story below.

Alexander Fleming and the Open Window

What do we learn about Fleming here?

Have you ever seen a slice of moldy bread? You probably thought it was pretty disgusting. Did you know, though, that a certain mold is one of the strongest medicines in the world? Penicillin, a medicine that kills dangerous bacteria, is made from *Pencillium notatum*, a rare mold. It's hard to imagine how anyone could think to use mold as medicine. One man did. His name was Alexander Fleming, and his discovery of penicillin is one of the most famous stories in the history of science. It begins with an open window…

It was a warm summer day in 1928, and a soft breeze blew into Dr. Alexander Fleming's laboratory in London, England. Dr. Fleming and his family were away on vacation. In his empty laboratory, countertops waited with flat glass dishes on them. The glass dishes had staphylococcus bacteria growing inside them. Dr. Fleming wanted to study these bacteria. In 1928, bacteria killed many people, and Fleming was trying to discover a way to stop them.

The curtains ruffled as a gentle wind carried in something unexpected. Tiny spores of penicillium mold danced in on the breeze and settled in the room. A few fell in the glass dishes full of bacteria. Then something amazing happened. The bacteria around the mold began to die, and no one was there to see it.

The next day, Alexander Fleming returned, ready to get back to work. He took the glass dishes full of bacteria to the sink to clean them. The penicillium mold was seconds away from being destroyed forever, when a knock sounded at the door. It was Merlin Pryce, a student who was also interested in learning about bacteria.

"How are your experiments going?" Pryce asked Fleming.

Fleming pulled some of the dishes from the sink. As he held out a dish to Pryce, he noticed something strange. "That's funny," he said, peering closely. Fleming noticed a white blob of mold, which seemed to be killing all the bacteria around it. Other scientists might have thrown the mold away, but Fleming had a theory. He had always believed that an antibiotic to

fight bacteria might be found in the unlikeliest of places. Over the years, he had tested all kinds of different substances, even saliva, to see if they could be an antibiotic cure against bacteria.

Fleming showed his dish to other scientists, but they didn't see how mold could be so important. Fleming decided to investigate anyway. He discovered what type of mold had settled in the dish, then he began experimenting. He took a sample of the mold and brewed "mold juice," a liquid soup with mold growing in it, which he later named penicillin. He tried his mold juice out on bacteria like streptococcus, pneumococcus, and meningococcus, all of which cause deadly infections. He discovered that the penicillin killed the bacteria, but there were problems. He couldn't get the penicillin to kill the bacteria fast enough. He wasn't sure if it would work inside the human body.

Fleming continued to experiment. Twelve years passed, when two scientists named Ernst Chain and Howard Florey were searching for an antibiotic, too. They remembered a rumor about a strange mold that could kill bacteria. Because Fleming had saved the mold all those years, they were able to experiment with it. Their experiments proved that Fleming had been on the road to discovering an amazing medical advance. Together, Fleming, Chain, and Florey made the "mold juice" into a medicine that could be used in hospitals. Their work has saved thousands and thousands of people all over the world.

In 1945, Alexander Fleming, Ernst Chain, and Howard Florey were awarded the Nobel Prize, the most important honor a scientist can receive. The discovery of penicillin involved not just luck, an open window, and a knock on the door, but also the open mind of Alexander Fleming.

We can learn more about what Fleming is like here.

Fleming investigated anyway. What does this tell us about him?

Look for a clue to what Fleming is like in this paragraph.

> **One way to describe Alexander Fleming is to say that he had an open mind. What does this expression tell you about Fleming? Use details from the article to explain your answer.**

Angela's Answer:

Here is Angela's answer. Read what she wrote. Then answer the questions that follow to see what makes her answer successful.

> If you say that Alexander Fleming had an open mind, you are saying something very important about him. "Open-minded" means that he didn't ignore anything. He stayed open to everything, even things that happened by accident. That's how he discovered the mold that we get penicillin from. While Fleming was away, the mold blew in the window of his laboratory and landed on some bacteria. Fleming saw the mold and realized that it had killed the bacteria. Because he had an open mind, he realized this might be important, even though he wasn't sure exactly how.
>
> Fleming's open mind led him to experiment with other bacteria to see if the mold would kill them, too. He still wasn't sure what to do with the mold. He didn't know whether it could be used to kill bacteria in a person. He didn't throw the mold away. He kept the mold, and he kept an open mind. Finally, working with two other scientists, he was able to find a way to make the mold into a life-saving medicine.

What Makes Angela's Answer Work?

Angela's answer has all the elements that the test scorers look for:

✓ She starts by stating her main idea.

✓ She gives relevant information from the selection to support her main idea.

✓ She connects her ideas in a logical way.

✓ She writes clear and interesting sentences.

Now let's take a closer look at Angela's answer to see what makes it work.

1. Angela's first two sentences restate the question and explain the main idea of her answer.

   Write Angela's opening sentences here. Underline the sentence in which Angela states the main idea.

   _____

   _____

   _____

   _____

2. In the first paragraph, Angela gives an example from the text that shows one way in which Alexander Fleming has an open mind.

   a. **First, find the two sentences that tell what happened in Fleming's laboratory. Write Angela's sentences here.**

   _____

   _____

   _____

   _____

   b. **Now find the sentence in Angela's answer that explains how this event shows that Fleming had an open mind. Write Angela's sentence here.**

   _____

   _____

   _____

3. In the second paragraph, Angela gives two more examples from the text to illustrate Fleming's open-mindedness.

   a. **What is the first example? Write Angela's sentence here.**

   _____

   _____

   _____

3. (continued)

   b. **What is the second example? Write Angela's sentence here.**

_____

_____

4. Angela's answer is easy to understand because she connected her ideas. They aren't organized randomly, but flow in a way that makes sense, from one idea to the next.

   Find a sentence in paragraph 2 that you think shows how Angela connects her ideas. Write Angela's sentence here.

_____

_____

5. Angela's sentences are interesting because she often combines ideas. Instead of short sentences that sound the same, she has some short, simple sentences and some long, complex sentences. Here is an example of a sentence where Angela has combined ideas to create a long, complex sentence: "While Fleming was away, the mold blew in the window of his laboratory and landed on some bacteria."

   Find another sentence in which Angela combines ideas. Write Angela's sentence here.

_____

_____

_____

_____

_____

Tools & Tips

In order to read between the lines, you need to make *inferences*. You need to think about the information in the selection and come up with your own ideas and explanations. The most important thing to remember is this:

The inference you make must be supported by the information in the selection.

Read the paragraph below and the inferences that follow. Decide which conclusion is best supported by the information in the paragraph.

Experiments on mice proved that penicillin killed bacteria and saved lives. It wasn't practical yet to use penicillin to cure infections in people. With *Penicillium notatum*, the kind of mold grown in the laboratory, doctors needed 2,000 liters of "mold juice" per patient. They also needed expensive equipment to extract and purify the penicillin.

INFERENCE 1: It took time and money to figure out a way to make the useful product we know as penicillin.

INFERENCE 2: Penicillin was an immediate success, saving many lives as soon as it was discovered.

Both Inference 1 and Inference 2 are about penicillin, but only Inference 1 is supported by information in the paragraph. Notice that the paragraph doesn't say time and money were needed to make penicillin an effective drug. You need to read between the lines to draw these conclusions. Which words in the paragraph are clues to this conclusion? Write the words below.

_____

_____

_____

_____

_____

Lesson 17

Strategy: Write a Good Opening

The first step when answering an open-ended question is to construct a good opening sentence. The sentence should:

✓ Repeat some or all of the questions being asked.

✓ Make a general statement of the main idea.

Look again Angela's answer. Compare it with the question.

> **One way to describe Alexander Fleming is to say that he had an open mind. What does this expression tell you about Fleming?**

Angela's Opening:

> If you say that Alexander Fleming had an open mind, you are saying something very important about him. "Open-minded" means that he didn't ignore anything.

In which sentence did Angela restate part of the question?

_____ a. sentence 1

_____ b. sentence 2

In which sentence did Angela make a general statement of the main idea?

_____ a. sentence 1

_____ b. sentence 2

Notice that Angela's general statement doesn't answer the question in detail. It states the main idea of her answer. She still needs to support that main idea, or general statement, with details from the reading selection.

A. Read these open-ended questions about the selection. Each one is followed by a two-sentence opening. For each opening, write **Q** next to the sentence that restates part or all of the **question**. Write **M** next to the sentence that states the **main idea**.

1. **Question:** How was Alexander Fleming different from other scientists?

   _____ a. Alexander Fleming was different from other scientists.

   _____ b. He was open to things that happened accidentally, like mold blowing in the window.

2. **Question:** What was so amazing about what happened in Fleming's laboratory?

   _____ a. Fleming wasn't looking for penicillin, but he discovered it by chance.

   _____ b. Something amazing happened in Fleming's laboratory.

3. **Question:** Why did Fleming keep the dish of mold?

    ____ a. Fleming kept a dish that had mold growing in it.

    ____ b. He saw something interesting in the dish that he wanted to study more.

4. **Question:** Why was the discovery of penicillin so important?

    ____ a. The discovery of penicillin was very important.

    ____ b. Scientists had been looking for something that could kill the bacteria that killed people.

5. **Question:** Why did it take so long to turn the mold into medicine?

    ____ a. At first, no one thought Fleming's discovery was very important.

    ____ b. It took a long time to turn the mold into medicine.

B. Try writing a good opening yourself. Reread Angela's question and her opening sentences. Rewrite Angela's opening in your own words.

Rewrite Angela's opening here.

_____

_____

_____

_____

_____

_____

_____

_____

_____

_____

HINT!

Make sure you include part or all of the question and a general statement that explains your main idea.

Lesson 18

Strategy: Choosing Relevant Details

Relevant details are information from the selection *that supports your main idea*. They're not just any old facts or details. The details must relate to the question. Relevant details are also called *supporting* details.

A. Read this paragraph, then answer the questions.

The discovery of penicillin was not the work of just one person. Alexander Fleming identified the mold that killed bacteria. Howard Florey and Ernst Chain began to experiment with penicillin to treat infections in people. It took a fourth person, a biochemist named Norman Heatley, to turn the "mold juice" into a medication that could be produced in large quantities in a factory.

1. Which sentence states the main idea of the paragraph?

_____

_____

_____

2. Are the details in the rest of the sentences all relevant? __ yes ___ no
3. What makes them relevant?

_____

_____

_____

B. Each sentence below states a main idea. The sentences that follow are details. Put a check mark next to the detail that is relevant to, or supports the main idea. Then explain why that detail is relevant.

1. **Main Idea:** An accident in Fleming's laboratory led to an important discovery.

_____ a. Fleming was studying the bacterium *Staphylococcus aureus*, which caused deadly infections in people.

_____ b. A mold blew in through the window and began to grow in the same dish as the bacteria Fleming was examining.

Why is it relevant?

_____

_____

2. **Main Idea:** The discovery that the penicillium mold would kill bacteria was just the first step in the development of the antibiotic penicillin.

      _____ a. Scientists needed to figure out exactly which ingredient in the penicillium mold killed bacteria.

      _____ b. A police officer in England died of an infection because there wasn't enough penicillin available to cure him.

Why is it relevant?

_____

_____

3. **Main Idea:** *Penicillium notatum* was not the only mold that could kill infections.

      _____ a. The mold on a cantaloupe was a gold color that the research assistant described as very pretty.

      _____ b. The mold on a cantaloupe, *Penicillium chrysogeum*, produced even more penicillin than the mold Fleming had discovered in his laboratory.

Why is it relevant?

_____

_____

4. **Main Idea:** An American woman was the first person whose life was saved by penicillin.

      _____ a. In 1942, she had an infection that had led to blood poisoning.

      _____ b. She was treated at New Haven Hospital in Connecticut.

Why is it relevant?

_____

_____

5. **Main Idea:** Although penicillin was considered a miracle drug, we know now that it isn't always effective.

      _____ a. It took lots of work before penicillin could be made in factories and be available in large quantities.

      _____ b. If penicillin is used too much, the bacteria become resistant to it and are not killed.

Why is it relevant?

_____

_____

Lesson 19

Strategy: Combine Sentences

Angela's answer was successful for many reasons. Here are two of them:

✓ She connected her ideas in a logical way.

✓ She wrote interesting sentences.

Writers do both of these things when they combine sentences. Combining sentences means combining ideas that might appear into short sentences to form a longer, more interesting sentence. When you join ideas in a sentence, you are also showing your reader how the ideas are connected.

A. Here is an example from Angela's answer.

> While Fleming was away, the mold blew in the window of his laboratory and landed on some bacteria.

This sentences combines the following ideas:

✓ Fleming was away.

✓ The mold blew in the window of his laboratory.

✓ It landed on some bacteria.

Read Angela's answer out loud. Then read the separate short sentences. What differences do you hear between the combined and the uncombined sentences?

B. Here are three ideas that could be combined into one sentence.

✓ He had an open mind.

✓ He realized this might be important.

✓ He wasn't sure exactly how.

1. Write one sentence that combines these three ideas. Try to use words that show how the ideas are connected.

   Write your answer here.

   _____

   _____

   _____

2. Compare the sentence you wrote with the one Angela wrote. (It's the last sentence of the first paragraph on page 104.) What words did Angela use to connect her ideas?

   Write them here.

   _____

C. Here are some additional ideas from the reading selection. Write a new sentence that combines each group of ideas. Try to use words that connect the ideas.

1. In Fleming's laboratory, there were some dishes. They were glass. Bacteria were growing in them.

_____

_____

_____

2. Fleming wanted to keep the bacteria. He wanted to study them. He hoped to find something that would kill the bacteria.

_____

_____

_____

3. Fleming had been on vacation. He had just returned. He was ready to get back to work.

_____

_____

_____

4. Fleming had a friend. His name was Merlin Pryce. Pryce was a student. He was interested in learning about bacteria.

_____

_____

_____

5. Fleming was getting ready to clean up his laboratory. Pryce knocked on the door. Pryce interrupted Fleming.

_____

_____

_____

Lesson 20

Revising and Improving a Weak Answer

You have analyzed an answer to see what makes it successful. Now you will learn how to revise and improve an answer that isn't successful. Reread the reading selection *Alexander Fleming and the Open Window*. Then read this question.

> **What role did chance play in Alexander Fleming's discovery of penicillin? Support your answer with details from the selection.**

Taylor's Answer:

Taylor tried to answer the question, but his answer was not successful. Read Taylor's answer. Remember what you have learned about a good answer. Use the questions that follow to help you revise and improve Taylor's answer.

> Chance played a big role in Alexander Fleming's discovery of penicillin. Fleming's lucky accident. It was just by chance that the penicillin mold started to grow in Fleming's laboratory. This story shows how important chance is.

Improving Taylor's Answer

Taylor has answered the question, but it is not very complete. He has included only one supporting detail, and he hasn't really explained the role that chance played in the discovery of penicillin. In addition, not all his sentences are complete. The test scorers would probably evaluate that Taylor needs to include more details and write better sentences to get a better score.

Answer the following questions to help revise and improve Taylor's score.

1. Did Taylor follow his opening sentence with a sentence that explains the main idea?

   If not, what does Taylor need to add to his opening? Write a new sentence here.

   _____

   _____

   _____

2. Taylor's second sentence is not complete. It's a fragment.

   How can Taylor complete this sentence? Write a new sentence here.

   _____

   _____

   _____

3. Has Taylor said enough about this step in the discovery of penicillin?

   If not, what should Taylor add to make his answer more complete? Write at least two new sentences with additional details.

   _____

   _____

   _____

   _____

4. Taylor's third sentence could be the end of a first paragraph.

   What sentence should Taylor write to introduce a second paragraph—a paragraph about a second way that chance played a role in Fleming's discovery of penicillin? Write a new sentence here.

   _____

   _____

   _____

5. What else should Taylor say about this step in the discovery of penicillin?

   Write at least two new sentences with additional details here.

   _____

   _____

   _____

   _____

6. Now that you've added more details to Taylor's answer, think about the closing sentence.

   How can Taylor change his last sentence to make it more interesting? Write a new closing sentence here.

   _____

   _____

   _____

SCORE BUILDER

Combining sentences does more than make your sentences more interesting. It also helps you avoid making these two mistakes: fragments and run-ons.

Fragments: A fragment is a group of words that looks like a sentence. It starts with a capital letter and ends with a period, but it is not complete. It is missing part of the thought. You can correct a fragment by combining it with another sentence:

✓ Fleming made his discovery. (complete sentence)

✓ Because he noticed the mold just in time. (fragment)

✓ Fleming made his discovery because he noticed the mold just in time. (complete sentence)

Run-ons: A run-on is two or more sentences that haven't been combined correctly. The two sentences have been jammed together without punctuation or connecting words. You can correct a run-on by adding the right punctuation or by adding a connecting word.

✓ Fleming pulled the dish out of the sink the mold was still there. (run-on)

✓ Fleming pulled the dish out of the sink; the mold was still there. (correct)

✓ Fleming pulled the dish out of the sink, and the mold was still there. (correct)

Fix these fragments and run-ons.

1. The window was open a mold blew in.

_____

_____

2. The mold landed in a dish. Where bacteria were growing.

_____

_____

Responding on Your Own

Here is a third question about the reading selection *Alexander Fleming and the Open Window*. This time you will answer the question on your own. As you plan and write your answer, think about what you have learned from analyzing Angela's answer and improving Taylor's answer. You should also use the following to help you write your answer:

✓ the **strategies** you practiced

✓ the tips you were given in **Tools & Tips**

✓ the reminders in the **Score Builde**

Read this question. You need to "read between the lines" of the reading selection to find the answer.

> **What qualities made Alexander Fleming a good scientist? Support your answer with your own ideas and with details from the selection.**

Write your answers on the lines below

_____
_____
_____
_____
_____
_____
_____
_____
_____
_____
_____
_____
_____
_____
_____

HINT!

Test scorers look for the following things:

✓ A clear and interesting opening.

✓ A complete answer to the question.

✓ Relevant details from the selection.

✓ A strong closing.

✓ Clear, complete, and interesting sentences.

Reader's Response!
Revise & Edit

When you have finished writing, exchange papers with a partner. As you read each other's answers, follow these steps.

1 Did the writer answer the question? ___ **Yes** ___ **No**

2 Was the opening clear and interesting? ___ **Yes** ___ **No**
If not, what needs to be changed?
Write your response here.

_____

_____

_____

3 Did the writer use relevant details from ___ **Yes** ___ **No**
the selection to support the main ideas?
If not, what needs to be added or changed?
Write your response here.

_____

_____

_____

_____

4 Are the writer's sentences correct and interesting? ___ **Yes** ___ **No**

5 Has the writer followed all the SLAMS rules? ___ **Yes** ___ **No**
If not, which rules were not followed?
Check all the boxes that apply.

S ___ L ___ A ___ M ___ S ___

6 **Give the paper back to your partner to revise and edit.**

Reviewing the Question

Remember that some questions ask you to read between the lines. They ask you to figure out things for yourself, to draw your own conclusions about the information in the reading selection. Here are some examples of open-ended questions that ask you to read between the lines. Pay attention to the words in bold type. Words like these signal that you are being asked to read between the lines.

- **How** did Fleming's open mind help him make an important discovery?

- **Why** were Chain and Florey's contributions to the development of penicillin so important?

- **What** qualities do you think a scientist should have?

- **Why** was the discovery of penicillin so important?

- **What** conclusions can you draw about the way scientists work?

Reading Beyond the Lines

What do experienced readers do as they read? Do they—

1. focus on understanding the big ideas and the facts?

2. understand what's happening when the author doesn't spell it out?

3. ask themselves and the author questions as they go along?

4. check the ideas or events against their own experiences?

The answer to all of the above is yes!

- When reading what's on the page, experienced readers concentrate on item 1.

- When reading between the lines, experienced readers focus on item 2.

- When reading beyond the lines, experienced readers apply items 3 and 4.

Experienced readers are *active*. As they read, it's like they are having a conversation with the author. Active reading encourages you to *bring yourself along* as you read, not just read the words.

Some test questions test your ability to make connections between what you read and your own ideas and experiences. Questions that test your ability to read beyond the lines might ask you to compare ideas with your own experiences or to tell about how you solved a similar problem. You might be asked to give your opinion about the ideas or the situation in a selection. Whatever the questions, remember to "bring yourself along." Ask yourself, "Has this ever happened to me? Do I think this is a good solution? Do I agree with the author?"

122

Lesson 22

What Makes a Good Answer?

Read the selection below. As you read it, think about your own experiences and knowledge.

Noisy Ghosts

Mrs. Fox clutched her husband. At three in the morning, everyone else in the farmhouse was asleep—or seemed to be. Eerie footsteps and knocks echoed through the house, and the sound of something heavy dragged across the floor, coming closer and closer. There was no question. The house was haunted!

In 1848, a small farmhouse was quickly becoming known as the most haunted place in New York State. At first, the ghostly presence made itself known only to Mr. and Mrs. Fox and their young daughters, Margaret and Kate, ages 13 and 11. As Mrs. Fox grew more and more frightened of the spirit's nightly visits, neighbors from miles around visited the farmhouse to hear the ghostly noises.

Imagine you lived near the farmhouse.

The Foxes grew concerned. The ghost seemed to like their daughters, and it seemed to want to communicate with them. Mysterious bumping and knocking sounds followed the girls wherever they went. The girls even worked out a code with the ghost. Two knocks from the ghost meant "no," and one knock meant "yes." When one bold visitor asked the ghost whether a murder had been committed in the house, a single chilling knock split the air like a gunshot. "Yes," the ghost had knocked.

News of the little Fox girls and their ability to speak to ghosts made newspapers across the world. The girls had an older sister named Leah. Leah realized that people would pay to see and hear them. She took charge of her sisters' careers and traveled with them across the United States, where they displayed their amazing powers in front of paying audiences.

Who do you believe? Why?

Not everybody believed that the Fox girls were speaking to ghosts. Three doctors examined the girls and decided that they had been making the noises themselves, perhaps by clicking together the bones in their knees. However,

other doctors, lawyers, and investigators who examined the girls disagreed. They firmly believed that the noises were ghostly in origin.

As the Fox girls' fame grew, imitators appeared. Many were skilled magicians. The minute they turned out the lights, furniture jumped and invisible instruments played haunting melodies. Glowing shapes would fly around the room, and some people in the audience might shriek because they thought they felt something touch their hair. To create these special effects, the magicians had a little help from hidden puppeteers and glow-in-the-dark paint. The Fox girls couldn't compete with such visually stunning shows, and the girls gradually lost their audiences.

Then in 1888, after many years, Margaret Fox made a startling announcement—it had all been a trick. There were no ghosts! For a price, she offered to reveal their secrets. She and her sisters had fooled everybody about the noises. The girls themselves had provided the sounds. To create the ghostly rapping, they had learned to snap the knuckles of their toes. Margaret even demonstrated her noisy toes in front of an audience of over two thousand people. To create the sound of something mysterious moving across the floor, they had tied an apple to a string and dragged it across the floor.

Despite Margaret's confession, many people still believed that she had talked to ghosts. Even today people still want to believe that some people can communicate with ghostly beings.

The answer to the noisy ghosts is revealed here!

Why might people want to believe in ghosts?

Read this open-ended question about the story. Notice that it asks you to include details from the selection and from your own experiences.

> **The Fox sisters and their imitators fooled people with tricks the way a magician does. Have you ever been fooled by a magician doing magic tricks? Compare your experience with the description in the selection.**

Emily's Answer:

Here is Emily's answer. Read what she wrote. Then answer the questions that follow to see what makes Emily's answer successful.

When I was young, I thought my dad was really magical. He could make coins disappear and make any card I thought of fly out of a deck of cards. I guess the people who watched the Fox sisters and their imitators must have felt like I did. Someone who could talk in code with ghosts or could make glowing figures fly around in the dark must have powers that ordinary people couldn't understand, just like I couldn't understand my dad's magic.

Of course, as I got older, I realized that my dad didn't have real magic powers. He was just good at tricking me, like the Fox girls were good at tricking their audiences. Dad wouldn't tell me how he did his tricks. Magicians don't, except to other magicians. So I thought maybe Dad really was a magician, sort of.

One day my dad bought me a present, a real magic trick I could do myself. I practiced and then tried it out on my mother. I was going to play a trick, just like my dad and the Fox girls had done. I asked my mom to make a mark on a dime, and I put the dime in my pocket. From my pocket, I pulled out a small red box closed tight with rubber bands. Mom took off all the rubber bands, and inside was a matchbox. From the matchbox she pulled out a small closed bag. She opened the bag, and inside was the marked coin.

"How did you do that, Emily?" she wanted to know. I didn't tell her. Magicians don't tell their secrets.

> **HINT!**
>
> No two people have exactly the same experiences or opinions. This question does not have one correct answer. How you respond depends on the experiences you have had as well as on your understanding of the story.

What Makes Emily's Answer Work?

Emily does exactly what the scorers look for:

✓ She tells her story clearly.

✓ She includes details from the reading selection in her answer.

✓ She adds ideas from her own experience as further support.

✓ She writes an interesting opening and closing.

Now let's take a closer look at Emily's answer to see what makes it successful.

1. A successful answer should have an interesting opening. A good opening gets the reader involved right away.

   Which sentence in Emily's first paragraph gets your attention and makes you want to read more? Write that sentence here.

   _____

   _____

   _____

2. Emily includes details from the selection to show that she has understood what she has read.

   In your own words, explain the details about the Fox girls and their imitators that Emily included. Write your response here.

   _____

   _____

   _____

   _____

3. Emily includes her own experiences. She mentions some magic tricks that fooled her as a child.

   What were the tricks that fooled her? Write Emily's sentence here.

   _____

   _____

   _____

4. Emily makes a direct connection between the events in the selection and her own feelings when she watched her dad perform a magic trick.

   How does Emily explain the connection? Write one of Emily's sentences here.

   _____

   _____

   _____

5. Eventually, Emily realized that magic tricks are just that—tricks, not real magic at all.

   How does Emily explain this change in her thinking? Write Emily's sentences here.

   _____

   _____

   _____

   _____

   _____

   _____

6. Finally, something happened that made Emily similar to the Fox girls.

   Explain what happened in your own words. Write your answer here.

   _____

   _____

   _____

   _____

   _____

Tools & Tips

Emily made a direct connection between her experience and the experiences in the selection. She made this connection by **comparing** herself to the people who were fooled by the Fox sisters and their imitators. Read the sentences below from Emily's answer. The words in bold type highlight the connection and the comparison.

✓ I guess the people who watched the Fox sisters and their imitators must have **felt like** I did.

✓ Someone who talked in code with ghosts or could make glowing figures fly around in the dark must have powers that ordinary people couldn't understand, **just like I couldn't understand** my dad's magic.

✓ I was going to play a trick, **just like my dad and the Fox girls had done**.

Read each pair of sentences. Write a sentence that connects each pair by comparing the two experiences.

1. **Emily's Experience:** Of course, as I got older, I realized that my dad didn't have real magic powers.

   Reading Selection: But not everybody believed that the Fox girls were actually speaking to ghosts.

   Connecting Sentence:

   _____

   _____

   _____

2. **Emily's Experience:** I thought my dad was really magical. He could make coins disappear and make any card I thought of fly out of a deck of cards.

   Reading Selection: She and her sisters had fooled everybody about the noises. It was the girls themselves providing the sounds.

   Connecting Sentence:

   _____

   _____

   _____

Lesson 23

Strategy: Use Your Own Experiences

When you read beyond the lines, you need to use your own experiences to help you understand the reading selection. That means you need to figure out which of your experiences relate to the events in the reading selection. Emily did this in her answer when she compared her feelings about her dad's magic tricks to the feelings of the people who saw the Fox girls' tricks.

To make a connection between a reading selection and your own life, you need to ask yourself such questions as:

✓ Has anything like this ever happened to me?

✓ Has anything like this ever happened to someone I know?

✓ Have I ever read about anything like this?

✓ Have I ever heard about anything like this?

✓ Have I ever seen anything like this on television or in the movies?

A. Read this question. It is the same one Emily answered.

> **The Fox sisters and their imitators fooled people with tricks the way a magician does. Have you ever been fooled by a magician doing magic tricks? Tell what happened, using details from the selection and from your own experience in your answer.**

Describe an experience of your own to answer this question. Write your answer here.

_____

_____

_____

_____

_____

_____

_____

_____

_____

_____

HINT!

You can use something that's happened to someone else or something you've read about if you can't think of an experience of your own.

B. Here are two more questions that ask you to include your experiences in the answer. For each question, describe an experience in your answer.

1. Why do you think the Fox girls and their imitators were able to fool people so easily? Use details from the selection and your own experiences in your answer.

   Write your answer here.

   _____

   _____

   _____

   _____

   _____

   _____

   _____

   _____

2. Have you ever fooled someone with a magic or another kind of trick, the way the Fox girls did? Explain what happened and why. Use details from the selection and your own experiences in your answer.

   Write your answer here.

   _____

   _____

   _____

   _____

   _____

   _____

   _____

   _____

HINT!

Make sure you connect your experience to the reading selection.

Lesson 24

Strategy: Explain Cause and Effect

The reading selection *Noisy Ghosts* has many examples of *cause* and *effect*, like these:

✓ Mr. and Mrs. Fox heard strange sounds in the middle of the night. They were sure ghosts were haunting the house.

✓ The Fox girls cracked the knuckles of their toes. People believed that ghosts were making the sounds.

✓ Magicians painted puppets with glow-in-the-dark paint. Audiences believed they saw flying ghosts.

In each example, the second event is the result of the first one. You can emphasize the cause and effect with the words *as a result*: Mr. and Mrs. Fox heard strange noises in the night; <u>as a result</u>, Mr. and Mrs. Fox were convinced they had heard ghosts. You can also emphasize cause and effect with the word *cause*: The strange noises they heard in the night <u>caused</u> Mr. and Mrs. Fox to believe that their house was haunted.

A. Reword the other two examples above to emphasize the cause-and-effect relationship.

1. _____

_____

_____

2. _____

_____

_____

B. Each pair of sentences below expresses a cause-and-effect relationship. Rewrite each pair twice. Use two different ways to show that one event is the cause and the other is the effect.

1. Margaret Fox tied a string around an apple and dragged it across the floor. Thousands of people thought they heard a ghost moving across the floor.

a. _____

_____

_____

b. _____

_____

_____

HINT!

Good readers:

✓ recognize cause-and-effect relationships;

✓ explain cause-and-effect relationships when they answer open-ended questions.

2. People heard that the Fox girls could communicate with ghosts. They began coming to the farmhouse at night to hear the sounds.

a._____

_____

_____

b._____

_____

_____

3. People didn't believe that the Fox girls could talk to ghosts. Doctors examined them.

a._____

_____

_____

b._____

_____

_____

4. Leah Fox, The older sister of Margaret and Kate, saw that audiences would pay to see her sisters. She put herself in charge of their careers.

a._____

_____

_____

b._____

_____

_____

HINT!

To vary your sentences, try starting them with "As a result of" or "Because."

Lesson 25

Strategy: Compare and Contrast

When you answer an open-ended question that asks you to include your own experiences, you are often comparing your experience to something in the reading selection. Read the questions below. Notice how they ask you to compare and contrast.

a. The Fox sisters and their imitators fooled people with tricks the way a magician does. Think of a time that you were fooled by a magician. How was your experience like the experience of the Fox sisters' audience? How was it different?

b. The Fox sisters and their imitators created special effects. What kinds of special effects have you seen in movies and on television? How are they similar to ones created by the Fox sisters and their imitators? How are they different?

c. Emily practiced and practiced until she could fool people with a real magic trick. Think of something that you practiced until you could do it perfectly. How was your experience like Emily's? How was it different?

In order to answer questions like these, you need to be able to:

✓ compare—explain the similarities

✓ contrast—explain the differences

Try it with the questions above. For each question, follow these steps:

1. Think of an experience—or something you are familiar with from books, movies, or television—to include in your answer. Notice that the first two questions ask you to make a connection to events in the reading selection. The last question asks you to make a connection to an event in Emily's response.

2. Decide how your experience is similar to and different from the one in the question.

3. Write a paragraph describing your experience. Compare and contrast to connect your experience to the one mentioned in the question.

Write your answers to the first question here.

_____

_____

_____

_____

_____

Write your answers to the second question here.

_____

_____

_____

_____

_____

_____

_____

_____

_____

Write your answers to the last question here.

_____

_____

_____

_____

_____

_____

_____

_____

_____

Lesson 26

Revising and Improving a Weak Answer

Now that you know strategies, try improving an answer that is not so successful. Return to pages 122 and 123 and read *Noisy Ghosts* again. Then read the open-ended question below.

> **Imagine you traveled back in time to 1848. Do you think you would have been fooled by the Fox sisters or their imitators? Include details from the selection and your own experience in your answer.**

Jack's Answer:

Read Jack's answer. Then use the questions that follow to help you improve it.

> I don't believe in ghosts. The imitators' tricks seem sort of cheesy. Maybe the Fox sisters would have fooled me, especially when they were in their own house at night.

Improving Jack's Answer

Jack has begun to answer the question. He explains that he doesn't believe in ghosts. He states that he wouldn't have been tricked by the imitators. He suggests that maybe the happenings in the Fox sister's house might have fooled him.

Jack's answer has a number of problems.

✓ He doesn't answer the question directly, so the reader isn't certain of what his answer is.

✓ His answer is much too short.

✓ He doesn't refer to details in the selection.

✓ He doesn't mention his own experiences to support his opinion.

Imagine that you wrote Jack's answer. Answer the following questions to help you revise and improve it.

1. Jack's answer is not clear. How can you change the opening sentence so it is clearer? **Write a new opening sentence or sentences here.**

_____

_____

_____

2. The second sentence mentions the imitators' tricks. What were some of these tricks? **Describe some of the tricks here.**

_____

_____

3. Jack's answer called the imitators' tricks "cheesy." That means Jack doesn't think much of them, but he does not say why.

   What was "cheesy" about the imitators' tricks? Write your answer here. Include details from your own experience.

   _____

   _____

   _____

   _____

   _____

4. The third sentence mentions events in the Fox sisters' house at night, but it doesn't include any details.

   What happened in the Fox sisters' house at night? Write your new sentences here. Include details from the selection.

   _____

   _____

   _____

   _____

5. Jack says that "maybe the Fox sisters would have fooled me, especially when they were in their own house at night."

   Would the Fox sisters have fooled you? Why? Write your reasons here. Include details from your own experience.

   _____

   _____

   _____

   _____

   _____

6. Look back at the changes you have made to improve Jack's answer.

   Rewrite Jack's entire answer on another sheet of paper. Be sure to include all the changes you made when you answered these questions.

SCORE BUILDER

A boy named Henry wrote the following paragraph. Read it.

It's always a big secret. They have these great tricks, but don't tell you how to do them. I'd like someone to show me how it works, just once. I don't think it would be such a big deal.

Do you know what Jason is writing about? His writing raises a lot of questions:

✓ What's a big secret?

✓ Who are "they"?

✓ Who or what are "them"?

✓ What's "it"?

✓ Is the "it" in the last sentence the "it" in the next-to-last sentence?

Words like *it* and *they* are very vague. Readers don't always know what person, thing, event, or idea these words refer to. Read Henry's revised paragraph below. Is it easier to understand?

Magic is always a big secret. Magicians have these great tricks, but they don't tell you how they do them. I'd like someone to show me how a trick works, just once. I don't think telling me would be such a big deal.

Compare the two paragraphs by answering these questions.

1. What does the first "it" refer to? What's a big secret?

_____

2. Who does "they" refer to at the beginning of the second sentence?

_____

Be careful when you use words like *they* and *it* in your writing. Make sure you have named the person, place, thing, event, or idea first before you use these words.

Responding on Your Own

Here is one more question about the reading selection *Noisy Ghosts*. This time you will answer on your own. As you plan and write your answer, think about what you have learned from analyzing Emily's answer and improving Jack's answer. You should also use the following to help you write your answer:

✓ the **strategies** you practiced

✓ the tips you were given in **Tools & Tips**

✓ the reminders in the **Score Builder**

Notice that this question, like the first two, asks you to read beyond the details in the story.

> **The Fox sisters started out by playing a kid's prank, but it got out of control. Think of a time when you started something that got out control. Tell about it, using details from the selection and your own experience in your answer.**

Write your answer on the lines below.

_____

_____

_____

_____

_____

_____

_____

_____

_____

_____

_____

_____

_____

_____

HINT!

As you read your answer, ask yourself these questions:

✓ Have I let my readers know what question I'm answering?

✓ Have I used details from the reading selection?

✓ Have I used details from my own experience?

✓ Have I written clear, complete sentences?

Reader's Response
Revise & Edit

When you have finished writing, exchange papers with a partner. As you read each other's answers, follow these steps:

1 Did the writer answer the question? ___ **Yes** ___ **No**

2 Did the writer explain the question in the opening? ___ **Yes** ___ **No**
If not, what needs to be added or changed?
Write your response here.

_____

_____

_____

3 Did the writer include relevant details from the selection? ___ **Yes** ___ **No**
If not, what needs to be added or changed?
Write your response here.

_____

_____

_____

4 Did the writer provide an example from his or her own experience? ___ **Yes** ___ **No**

5 Has the writer followed all the SLAMS rules? ___ **Yes** ___ **No**
If not, which rules were not followed?
Check all the boxes that apply.

S __ L __ A __ M __ S __

6 **Give the paper back to your partner to revise and edit.**

Reviewing the Question

It's easy to recognize open-ended questions that ask you to read beyond the lines. These questions ask you directly about yourself. For example:

- What is **your** opinion of the Fox sisters?

- What would **you** have done if you had been in their position?

- Have **you** ever had an experience like theirs? What happened?

- Do **you** think it was better to keep on fooling people or to admit what they had done? Why?

Remember! When you are asked to read **beyond the lines**, you need to include details both from your own experience and from the reading selection.

Song Catcher

by Erin Bad Hand

Erin Bad Hand's heritage is part Native American and part European. She is Lakota on her father's side and Cherokee and Italian on her mother's side. She is a sun-dancer and singer with her family's drum group, Heart Beat. The song she is about to tell you was sung by her mother at the International Women's Conference in Beijing, China in 1999.

I was so excited! I had caught a fly ball! I…had caught…a song! I had all these words buzzing in my head! So, after school, I ran to our garage to find my dad, and I asked him to help me translate the words into Lakota. That night, I called and asked my uncle to help me create a melody to go with the words.

When Earth Day came, on that dazzling day in April, my family went to the celebration at the park. My mom and dad were there, and my sisters and brother. My uncles Tom and Richard, and the rest of my extended Heart Beat family were also there—ready to provide the music and the songs for dancing at the festival.

I knew everyone there, and I have always felt comfortable and at home singing at this festival. This time was different. I was going to sing the song I had caught. When the music began, my dad nodded to me. My hands were sweaty as I picked up my drumstick, and we began to pound out the rhythm. My dad took the lead. I held my breath and then began to sing with him. We sang the song over and over, in the Lakota way. We sang the song that came to me, the song I caught.

It was a profound experience, one in which I felt, for the first time, truly part of the musical tradition of my people. In the past I had been the listener, or the dancer, or the singer of other people's songs, but now I sang the song I had caught, and I gave it to my people, where it would stay forever.

My name is Erin Bad Hand. I am a song catcher. I come from a long line of song catchers and keepers, stretching back for generations on my father's side. It was his knowledge and his traditions that I grew up with, the traditions of the Lakota people.

We are a Native American tribe from the plains of South Dakota. Singing and catching songs are very important in our culture. It is through song that the culture is passed on. There are songs for birthdays, for naming babies, for reaching puberty. There are songs for death and dying and songs for sacred ceremonies. There are honoring songs for mothers, fathers, relatives, friends, and children. We also sing honoring songs for the Earth, our Mother.

The song I had caught was a song cherishing Mother Earth.

What is it to "catch" a song? Well, it is exactly that: to be walking along one day, minding your own business and suddenly catch a song as if it were a fly ball in a baseball game. It sounds silly, doesn't it? It is strange to think of a song as a thing you can catch and hold. Songs that are caught sometimes just end up in your head, and you don't know where they came from.

I was 12 years when I caught this song. I thought it was important to do something special to give special thanks to Mother Earth because the Lakota people believe that the earth is sacred. We call her Unci Maka, which means "Grandmother Earth." She gives life to the people, and we should honor her, respect her, and take care of her. I wanted to give her something but I was not sure what that was going to be.

Then, as I was walking that day, the words of this song came to me. It was as if I had an imaginary glove held open, and I was just standing around when I caught a fly ball.

Come,
Come,
Grandmother is singing
On behalf of her children,
She is singing.
She is living, we are helping her and
We will hear her.

In Lakota, it reads like this

Upo,
Upo,
Unci lowan yelo
Cinca un tantahan,
Lowan yelo.
Niunki, o unkiyapi nan
Naunhunpi ktelo.

I never thought that I would catch a song, even though my father and my uncles were all song catchers. The songs they taught me were their songs. I didn't know if I would ever catch a song.

Then one day I did.

1 Reading What Is on the Page ························

Erin says that songs are very important to the Lakota people. What details from the selection support this statement?

_____

_____

_____

_____

_____

_____

_____

_____

_____

_____

_____

_____

_____

_____

_____

_____

_____

_____

_____

_____

2 Reading Between the Lines ....

Erin says that she had always felt comfortable singing before the people at the Earth Day festival. However, when she began to sing her own song, she was very nervous. Why do you think she was nervous? Use details from the selection and your own ideas to support your answer.

_____

_____

_____

_____

_____

_____

_____

_____

_____

_____

_____

_____

_____

_____

_____

_____

_____

_____

_____

_____

_____

3 Reading Beyond the Lines ••••••••••••••••••••••••••••••••

Becoming a song catcher was an important part of growing up in the Lakota tradition. What family or cultural traditions are part of your life? Tell about a tradition that you have participated in. Why was it important to you and your family? Remember to use details from the selection and from your own experience in your answer.

_____

_____

_____

_____

_____

_____

_____

_____

_____

_____

_____

_____

_____

_____

_____

_____

_____

_____

_____

_____